ArtScroll Mesorah Series®

Expositions on Jewish liturgy and thought

Rabbis Nosson Scherman / Meir Zlotowitz
General Editors

aseres
hadibros

aseres
hadibros

THE TEN COMMANDMENTS/A NEW TRANSLATION
WITH A COMMENTARY ANTHOLOGIZED FROM
TALMUDIC, MIDRASHIC, AND RABBINIC SOURCES.

Published by

Mesorah Publications, ltd

Translation and Commentary by
Rabbi Avrohom Chaim Feuer

An Overview / "Prelude to Sinai," by
Rabbi Nosson Scherman

FIRST EDITION
First Impression ... February, 1981

This specially commissioned edition
is available in U.S.A. and Canada
from:
YESHIVATH BETH MOSHE
Milton Eisner Yeshiva
930 Hickory Street
Box 1141
Scranton, Pennsylvania 18505
(717) 346—1747

This volume in the
ARTSCROLL MESORAH SERIES®
is one of an ongoing project of works on Scripture,
Mishnah, liturgy, and classic
rabbinic literature and thought
published by
MESORAH PUBLICATIONS, Ltd.

Write for a full catalogue.

ISBN
0-89906-179-6 (hard cover)
0-89906-180-X (paper back)

סְדֵּר בְּמִסְדָּרֶת
חֶבְרַת אַרְטְסְקרול בע״מ

Typography by Compuscribe at ArtScroll Studios, Ltd.
1969 Coney Island Ave. / Brooklyn, N.Y. 11223 / (212) 339-1700

❧ An Overview / Prelude to Sinai

An Overview /
Prelude to Sinai

בְּהוֹצִיאֲךָ אֶת הָעָם מִמִּצְרַיִם תַּעַבְדוּן אֶת הָאֱלֹהִים
עַל הָהָר הַזֶּה

*When you [Moses] take the people out
from Egypt, you will [all] serve God at this
mountain (Exodus 3:12).*

אָמַר ר' אֶלְעָזָר, בְּשָׁעָה שֶׁהִקְדִּימוּ יִשְׂרָאֵל 'נַעֲשֶׂה'
לְ'נִשְׁמָע' יָצְתָה בַת קוֹל וְאָמְרָה לָהֶן: מִי גִילָה
לְבָנַי רָז זֶה שֶׁמַּלְאֲכֵי הַשָּׁרֵת מִשְׁתַּמְּשִׁין בּוֹ ...
בְּרֵישָׁא 'עוֹשֵׂי' וְהָדָר 'לִשְׁמוֹעַ'

*R' Elazar said: At the time Israel said 'we
will do' before [saying] 'we will listen' (Exodus 24:7), a Heavenly voice went forth
and said of them, 'Who revealed to My
children this secret that is used by the
ministering angels [who are described in
Psalms 103:20] ... first "they do" and then
"they listen"!' (Shabbos 88a)*

I. Potential and Impetus

*Redemption
Merited*

When God first revealed Himself to Moses with
the command that the reluctant shepherd
become the leader who would redeem enslaved Israel
from Egypt, Moses objected quite logically, 'Even if I
am worthy to be Your agent, why does Israel deserve
the miracle of the Exodus?' (See *Rashi, Exodus* 3:11.)

*Israel's merit lay
dormant, but not
dead.*

God, who spoke to Moses from the slopes of Sinai,
replied that Israel's merit lay dormant, but not dead.
Within two months of their liberation, the Jews
would surround Sinai and accept the Torah, an un-

dertaking, that would justify the past and future history of the universe. Its very existence was conditional upon Israel's willingness to accept the Torah; that was God's purpose and only Israel's dedication to the Torah could give life and meaning to creation *(Shabbos* 88a).

So Moses' view of Israel was true only superficially. He saw it as an enslaved nation that had been dragged down into the slime of idolatry and impurity, but God looked at slaves mixing mortar and baking bricks and saw the untainted spiritual potential that would be revealed at Mount Sinai when the Ten Commandments were given and further fulfilled in great Torah academies and lonely vigils with the sacred books of Talmud, codes, comment, and responsa. *You will serve God at this mountain (Exodus* 3:12) — that was sufficient merit for the redemption *(Rashi).*

God looked at slaves mixing mortar and baking bricks and saw the untainted spiritual potential that would be revealed at Mount Sinai.

Ramban explains that Moses wondered why Israel would be willing to follow him through a harsh desert and into a series of difficult battles with the martial kings of Canaan. Freedom, yes! — but why hardship and travail? God responded that Israel's reluctance would last only until it accepted the Torah at Sinai. Once the people declared their willingness to hear God's word and came to understand its depth and significance, no hurdle would be too inconvenient. For a trivial goal, any hardship is great; for a great goal, any hardship is trivial.

For a trivial goal, any hardship is great; for a great goal, any hardship is trivial.

Rashi and *Ramban* give us two concepts; both are true and they flow naturally one from the other. The Exodus was possible because the nation of Israel had retained the capacity to raise itself from the moral morass of Egypt and accept the Torah at Sinai; having accepted the Torah, they would gain insight, inspiration, and resolve — and be ready for greater sacrifice in pursuit of enhanced achievement. Aspiration and accomplishment nourish one another. The Sages say 'one who has one hundred *zuz* wants to have two hundred' *(Koheles Rabbah* 1:34). This applies to all areas of human activity. Just as the businessman wants to double his holdings, the

Aspiration and accomplishment nourish one another.

scholar wants to double his knowledge, the *tzaddik* wants to double his good deeds.

But before we can take this sort of ambition for granted, there must be an essential prerequisite: one must have the ambition to succeed. Many people are content to scrounge a simple livelihood, and have no desire for more. Many a student seeks no more knowledge than he needs to pass his tests and win his certificate. In trying to understand Israel as it left Egypt, we must ask a crucial question: Would the former slaves be content with freedom from physical oppression, or would they aspire to scale spiritual heights? Indeed, this is the crux of *Ramban's* comment. Moses wondered why the newly-freed nation would consent to the ordeal of going all the way to Canaan, through wilderness and war. God answered that the key would be the initial response. They need go only to Mount Sinai to receive the Torah. Having done that, their ambition for spiritual advance would have no limits. For Israel to rise to the demands of God and the Torah, they would have to make the first effort that would lead to further impetus. Would they?

In trying to understand Israel as it left Egypt, we must ask a crucial question: Would the former slaves be content with freedom from physical oppression, or would they aspire to scale spiritual heights?

The Real Person

In a very real sense, a human being is what he thinks and what he desires, for the essence of man is not his body but his soul.

In a very real sense, a human being *is* what he thinks and what he desires, for the essence of man is not his body but his soul. Human brute force can be replaced by animals and machines, the contribution of his strength is transitory. What is great in man and enduring in his legacy is the product of his mind and heart. Whatever preoccupies his intelligence and fires his passion at any given moment is the essential person at that particular instant. The sacred writings frequently say of the very righteous, שְׁכִינָה מְדַבֶּרֶת מִתּוֹךְ גְּרוֹנוֹ, *the Shechinah [Divine Presence] speaks from his throat;* the person who lives, breathes, and thinks the word and will of God becomes a conduit for his Maker's utterance. The throat and mouth are his, but the speech is God's, so to speak. Conversely, רְשָׁעִים בְּחַיֵּיהֶם קְרוּיִים מֵתִים, *the wicked are called corpses even in their lifetimes (Berachos 18b)* because people who occupy themselves with 'dead,' impure, impermanent matters are themselves without meaningful life (*Tzidkas HaTzaddik* 144).

It is true that Israel on the threshold of freedom was light years away from Sinai. In the expression of the Sages, they were already at the forty-ninth level of spiritual contamination and in imminent danger of falling to the fiftieth — and lowest — level, from which escape would have been impossible. But in its *aspirations*, Israel stood at Sinai. It wanted greatness. It wanted to be worthy of its forefathers and it had high ambitions for its posterity. And when it experienced Sinai it would be ready for even greater things, so it was worthy of redemption even then.

In its aspirations, Israel stood at Sinai. It wanted greatness. It wanted to be worthy of its forefathers and it had high ambitions for its posterity.

II. To Do and To Listen

Secret of Angels

On the fifth of Sivan, two days before the Ten Commandments were given, Israel told Moses of its willingness to obey God's word, saying, כֹּל אֲשֶׁר דִּבֶּר ה׳ נַעֲשֶׂה וְנִשְׁמָע, *whatever HASHEM speaks, we will do and we will listen* (*Exodus* 24:7; see *Rashi* there and *v.* 4). It was this declaration that prompted the Heavenly exclamation quoted by R' Elazar (*Shabbos* 88a), 'Who revealed to My children this secret that is used by the ministering angels!' For the angels, too, are described by the Psalmist (103:20) as creatures who first pledge to do, and who listen afterwards.

Surely logic agrees with the Sadducee who ridiculed Israel as 'an impetuous nation who put its mouth before its ears.'

Surely logic agrees with the Sadducee (*Shabbos* 88a) who ridiculed Israel as 'an impetuous nation who put its mouth before its ears ... first you should have listened [to the contents of the proposed Torah] — if you have found it acceptable, you should have taken it, and if not, you should have rejected it.' In order to agree that his point seems valid, we need not subscribe to the attitude of a Sadducee whose intention was more to blaspheme than to understand. Wouldn't Israel's response have been more meaningful if it had been based on knowledge and analysis rather than a blind acceptance of the unknown? What is meant by 'we will do'? Can one act

Wouldn't Israel's response have been more meaningful if it had been based on knowledge and analysis rather than a blind acceptance of the unknown?

before hearing what he is to do? Why is Israel's acceptance described as the attribute of angels, and why is this behavior called the 'secret' of the angels?

At the outset, let us understand clearly that Israel did not simply parrot the verbal formula of angels. R' Elazar says that the secret was *revealed* to them. The implication is clear: Israel comprehended the import of what it said. Had the people merely repeated a phrase used by angels, then words would have been empty sounds and certainly would not have elicited God's proud approval. The *Zohar* and *Ramban* frequently explain difficult, esoteric Kabbalistic ideas and conclude, 'this matter is a secret.' A secret? — but they have already explained the secret! The answer is simple. One can be taught to recite profound words but unless he comprehends the full depth of what he says, it remains a secret, even to the one who repeats it. A child can be taught to declaim a passage of *Zohar* with eloquence and passion, but it will remain as hidden from him as it was the day before he heard of it. But to Israel, the secret was *revealed;* when Israel used the formula of the angels, it touched the level of heavenly beings. Ordinary Jews had found the secret and assimilated its meaning. They were angels on earth *(R' Gedalia Schorr)*.

One can be taught to recite profound words but unless he comprehends the full depth of what he says, it remains a secret, even to the one who repeats it.

To Sublimate Self

An angel exists only to accomplish the purpose for which it was created. It has no inclinations, good or evil, no private desires or conflicts. That it wishes to perform its assigned task is because that wish, too, is part of its being. If we could imagine a hammer with intelligence and the power to move independently, it would surely travel from nail to nail, doing its job of pounding. It would ignore screws and surely not attempt to prepare food. It is a hammer and it will do whatever hammers must do, conscientiously and efficiently, but nothing more. An angel is truly that sort of being, albeit a spiritual one. Created for a particular purpose, it requires no persuasion or even information. It functions.

If we could imagine a hammer with intelligence and the power to move independently, it would surely travel from nail to nail, doing its job of pounding.

Man is different. He listens, thinks, calculates, and decides. He will do what is in his interest, what he enjoys, what he must — but he can freely refuse to do what displeases him. A human being is praiseworthy if he hears the teachings of the Torah and, after weighing them in the scales of his self-interest, decides that he prefers the service of God to all other considerations. But Israel did much more. As the people stood at Sinai they made the extraordinary decision to negate themselves totally to the wishes of God. They would be His hammers, His agents, His angels, the extensions of His will. By so deciding, Israel placed itself on the level of the angels, for it declared itself to be God's unquestioning servant, who dedicates his very existence solely to the service of his Master.

But Israel did much more. They would be His hammers, His agents, His angels, the extensions of His will.

How sharp the contrast between Israel and the other nations. The Sages teach that the Torah was available to every nation on earth, but no one would accept it. Bloody Edom could not accept a Torah that forbade bloodshed, thieving Ishmael wanted no part of a Torah that forbade stealing, licentious Moab could recognize no law without adultery, and so on (*Avodah Zarah* 2b; *Sifri*; *Brachah*).

Bloody Edom could not accept a Torah that forbade bloodshed, thieving Ishmael wanted no part of a Torah that forbade stealing.

Obviously, God did not somehow present each nation with a formal proposal to deliberate at conclaves of elders. The Torah was 'offered' in the sense that it was available to any nation that was willing to subjugate its desires to a Higher Intelligence and to dedicate itself to assimilating holiness into its daily affairs. In the long list of 613 commandments there are surely many that came hard to the individual Jew — can any of us claim to be totally as God would wish us to be, or even as *we* would wish ourselves to be? Nevertheless we are more than mere biological offspring of the people who said 'we will do.' Israel remains the *nation* that declares its willingness to be at God's service. It had that trait within it in Egypt, during its earliest sojourn at the lowest rungs of impurity. That quality endures (*Tiferes Yisrael*).

Israel remains the nation that declares its willingness to be at God's service. That quality endures.

Israel's Listening

In expressing that readiness, Israel did not neglect to say נִשְׁמָע, *we will listen,* for the people had an equal zeal to hear, study, and comprehend the words of

Torah. On the surface this would seem to be merely the practical necessity of learning what to do; first they volunteered, then they asked for instructions. But *Vilna Gaon (Aderes Eliyahu, Deuteronomy 5:24)* explains that this is not so. It is certainly vital to learn details of the *mitzvos*, but that was not what the Jews had in mind when they proclaimed 'we will listen.' Rather they signified a desire to *understand*, to plumb the depths of God's word.

It is certainly vital to learn details of the mitzvos, but that was not what the Jews had in mind when they proclaimed 'we will listen.'

The word שְׁמַע, *hear* or *listen*, represents more than the capacity to absorb information through the ears. When the Torah says שְׁמַע יִשְׂרָאֵל, *Hear O Israel, HASHEM our God, HASHEM is One*, it asks for more than the attention of the listeners. It asks us to show insight and conviction, to interpret events and order our lives in accordance with the overriding fact of HASHEM's Oneness.

The story is told of a man who left his family for an extended stay in the court of the Maggid of Mezritch, the successor of the Baal Shem Tov. Upon returning home, his skeptical and unsympathetic father-in-law demanded to know what he had accomplished there to justify the neglect of his family.

'In Mezritch, I learned that there is a God.'

The father-in-law scoffed and summoned the maid from the kitchen. 'Do you know that there is a God?' he asked.

'Of course, I know, sir,' she laughed. 'Everyone knows.'

The angry father-in-law bellowed, 'You deserted your family for Mezritch to learn something that even an illiterate maid could have told you!'

'She says there is a God, but in Mezritch I learned to know that there is a God.'

The wayward son-in-law replied simply, 'She *says* there is a God, but in Mezritch I learned to *know* that there is a God.'

This is the sort of 'listening' Israel had in mind when it responded to Moses. It is no coincidence that the Torah portion of the Ten Commandments begins with the words וַיִּשְׁמַע יִתְרוֹ, *and Jethro heard*. Jethro, Moses' father-in-law, left his privileged position in

Midian to rendezvous with Israel in the Wilderness because he heard all that God had done for Moses and Israel. Countless thousands had heard what had happened in Egypt, at the Sea of Reeds, and in the war with Amalek — but only Jethro came to cast his lot with Israel. Clearly, it is the *quality* of hearing that matters. Others heard and went about their daily affairs as if God had introduced no new factor into history. Jethro heard and comprehended — so he came.

Others heard and went about their daily affairs as if God had introduced no new factor into history. Jethro heard and comprehended — so he came.

By citing Jethro's type of hearing to introduce the momentous chapter of the Ten Commandments, the Torah prepares us to understand its concept of שְׁמִיעָה, *listening.* Especially in the modern world, we are all inundated by sounds and messages. Some we ignore, others we hear, a few we assimilate, but only a rare one in a lifetime truly changes us. Jethro *heard* — and he became a Jew. Israel resolved to do *and* to listen. What was the significance of their undertaking to listen?

We are all inundated by sounds and messages. Some we ignore, others we hear, a few we assimilate, but only a rare one in a lifetime truly changes us.

The angels, too, listen after they perform:

עֹשֵׂי דְבָרוֹ לִשְׁמֹעַ בְּקוֹל דְּבָרוֹ

They do His word, to listen to the sound of His word (Psalms 103:20)

In this context, 'to listen' is to obtain knowledge and understanding of the inner meaning of the acts that have been performed. For example, one may know and perform such commandments as studying Torah, giving proper tithes, redeeming firstborn sons, offering sacrifices of firstborn sheep and cattle, and consecrating first fruits. On a deeper level of understanding one may recognize that the Torah uses the word רֵאשִׁית, *first,* in connection with each of these commandments. This word implies the meaning that attaches to each of these *mitzvos.* By segregating the first — the foremost — of one's children and possessions for God's service and by contributing the first selections of crops toward the sustenance of God's servants, the Jew assimilates the message that his first accomplishments — the ones human nature understandably wishes to hoard for oneself and his loved ones — should be devoted

By contributing the first selections of crops, the Jew assimilates the message that his first accomplishments should be devoted toward a higher purpose.

toward a higher purpose. Instead of putting himself and his family above all other considerations, the Jew gives first priority to God, Torah and commandments.

God, too, acts on this premise. Israel is called רֵאשִׁית, the *foremost* among nations and the Torah is called רֵאשִׁית דַּרְכּוֹ, *the beginning of His way.* Because this nation would forgo its desires for the sake of His priorities, and dedicate itself to accept, study, and cherish His Torah, God created heaven and earth. As the Sages taught, the first word of the Torah בְּרֵאשִׁית, *In the beginning of,* is Midrashically interpreted as a contraction of בִּ[שְׁבִיל] רֵאשִׁית, *because of the things called* [רֵאשִׁית] *'the first,'* God created heaven and earth. (See *Rashi* to *Genesis* 1:1.) In this illustration of finding a common denominator in a list of commandments and tracing them back to God's initial motive, we have an inkling of what it means to *perform* a commandment, and then to go below the surface and search out its deeper meaning.

We have an inkling of what it means to perform a commandment, and then to go below the surface and search out its deeper meaning.

Defining Goals

The person who is trapped between personal desires, obligations, demands, mores of society, and conflicting professional values finds it difficult, if not impossible, to develop a consistent unified philosophy of life and action. How can he? He understands his need for self-gratification, and his obligation to God, and the need to sacrifice for spouse and children, and the requirements to adhere to the tenets of his profession. The average man is torn by many conflicting allegiances, but the נַעֲשֶׂה, *we-will-do*-person has only one. Because he knows that his allegiance belongs to One alone, he can 'hear' with more receptive ears and learn to reconcile everything he does with the paramount factor in his life.

Once a being has become dedicated to the performance of God's wishes — whether by creation like an angel or by choice like Israel at Sinai — the dedication gives birth to a new dimension of understanding. For a *fait accompli* creates a logic of its own.

Dedication gives birth to a new dimension of understanding. For a fait accompli creates a logic of its own.

This concept is not at all esoteric. There are brilliant people who master the details of scores of knotty problems. But because they have no guiding philosophy of life, they are doomed to wrestle with one triviality after another. If only they knew where they were going and what they wanted to accomplish, they could evaluate each isolated problem and decision on the basis of how well it fit into their guiding philosophy. Will a step bring them closer to their goals? — take it! Will it conflict with the main purpose? — avoid it!

So it was with Israel. At Sinai, the nation made a decision to serve God, then it could go on to listen and to understand everything in terms of how much it was in tune with God's will. The adoption of a philosophy creates a reality by which everything else is judged. We never wonder about the validity of the law of gravity because we know no other law, so we automatically reject any decision that will require us to walk off rooftops. Israel decided never to question the law of God, so it was free to understand it without giving credence to any conflicting course. Thanks to this decision, we can understand not only the Torah, but fit every experience into the frame of reference provided by our commitment to do God's will.

We never wonder about the validity of the law of gravity because we know no other law, so we automatically reject any decision that will require us to walk off rooftops.

III. Free-Willed Coercion

אָמַר רַב אַבְדִּימִי ... כָּפָה עֲלֵיהֶם הַר כְּגִיגִית
וְאָמַר לָהֶם אִם אַתֶּם מְקַבְּלִים הַתּוֹרָה מוּטָב וְאִם
לָאו שָׁם תְּהֵא קְבוּרַתְכֶם

Rav Avdimi said ... [when God gave the Ten Commandments] He [God] suspended Mount [Sinai] over them like a barrel and said, 'If you accept the Torah — good. But if not — there, your grave will be!' (Shabbos 88a)

Accepting the Condition

Tosefos *(ad loc)* raises an obvious difficulty. In view of Israel's enthusiastic — even angelic — acceptance of the Torah, why was it necessary for God to introduce the element of compulsion into the giving of the Torah? Various answers are offered, two of which flow from the above discussion.

Maharal differentiates between the time before Israel said 'we will do and we will listen' and afterward. Just as every people on earth had the option of accepting the Torah, but was unsuited or unwilling to do so, Israel had the right to accept or reject, and the nation transcended human logic. Instead of listening and deciding, Israel rose to the level of the angels and voluntarily became instruments of God's will. As we have seen, the very act of creation was based on the premise that the Torah would be the basis for human behavior — if not for all humanity than, at least, for Israel. As the Talmud *(ibid)* puts it, God created the universe on the condition that it could endure only if Israel were to accept the Torah; otherwise the entire vast universe would disappear and return to the total vacuum that existed before creation. Once Israel accepted that responsibility upon itself there was no turning back. A pilot may refuse to take up a flight if he wishes, but once he is in the stratosphere he cannot exercise his freedom of choice in mid-flight. By suspending the mountain over Israel, God showed us that we had indeed elected to become the 'angels' who serve Him and that creation exists in our merit. From that moment onward, we could no longer lay down the burden.

Once Israel accepted that responsibility upon itself there was no turning back. From that moment onward, we could no longer lay down the burden.

Insuring the Future

R' *Gedaliah Schorr* (see also *Chiddushei HaRim* cited in *Siach Sarfei Kodesh* II) likens Israel at Sinai to a person subject to fits of temporary insanity. While he is lucid, he urges his friends to restrain him if he becomes violent or destructive during his periods of illness. Someone who sees him in a strait jacket or being held down forcefully might conclude that he is being kidnaped or mugged, but those who know the facts are aware that his *own* will — as expressed when he was capable of making rational decisions — is being carried out.

The same was true of Israel at Sinai. In an extraordinary feat that remains a model of man's capacity for spiritual advancement, the nation had pulled itself up to the level of the angels from the moral decadence of Egyptian culture and the physical debilitation of slavery. But people can rarely remain in such a state of spiritual exaltation forever, or even for long. Indeed, it was only several weeks later that Israel itself asked Aaron to build it a golden god to lead and inspire it. In its most resplendent hour, the moment of supreme national lucidity, Israel sought a means to preserve that commitment even at times when its spiritual resources would be wanting. Intelligent people always search for ways to maintain their level of performance even when conditions are not ideal; Israel did the same and God provided assistance. By suspending the mountain over the nation, so to speak, God obliged Israel's most noble instincts by reinforcing its desire with compulsion.

In its most resplendent hour, the moment of supreme national lucidity, Israel sought a means to preserve that commitment even at times when its spiritual resources would be wanting.

This explains why similar means were not employed to coerce other nations to accept the Torah. God coerces only those who wish to submit. That Israel was 'forced' to accept the Torah is the supreme testimony and tribute to the strength of its convictions.

That Israel was 'forced' to accept the Torah is the supreme testimony and tribute to the strength of its convictions.

It is a principle of Jewish faith that our greatest moments are our norm. Israel was conceived in the heroic efforts of the Patriarchs and Matriarchs, the prophecies of Moses, the faith of little people, and a unanimous striving to graft the constancy of angels onto the frailty of man. We stumble and fall, but we must not fail to be inspired by the knowledge that an entire nation — not an occasional inspired Jew, but every man, woman, and child — rose to a level beyond human expectation and made that the standard by which Israel would always be judged.

Israel remains at Sinai, and God Himself pays homage to His children whose conviction was powerful enough to uncover the secret of the angels.

In the depths of its soul, Israel remains at Sinai, and God Himself pays homage to His children whose conviction was powerful enough to uncover the secret of the angels.

Rabbi Nosson Scherman

עשרת הדברות

וַיְדַבֵּר אֱלֹהִים אֵת כָּל־הַדְּבָרִים הָאֵלֶּה א
לֵאמֹר: ב אָנֹכִי יהוה אֱלֹהֶיךָ אֲשֶׁר

1. וַיְדַבֵּר אֱלֹהִים — *God spoke.*

When Moses informed the Jewish people that God intended to give them the Torah at Sinai, their enthusiasm was boundless. Their immediate response was, *'All that HASHEM has said, we will do and we will listen' (Exodus* 24:7); so complete was their faith in God and in the goodness of His dictates that they proclaimed their readiness to 'do' even before they heard what would be demanded of them (see Overview).

However, the Children of Israel had one urgent request: רְצוֹנֵנוּ לִרְאוֹת אֶת־מַלְכֵּנוּ, *it is our desire to see* [as it were] *our King.* Much though they revered Moses, they wished to experience the awesome revelation of a direct communication from God Himself. God acquiesced. Unlike mortal kings who address their subjects through ministers and heralds, at Sinai, God spoke directly to each man, woman, and child.

Israel earned this remarkable display of affection, measure for measure, because of the devotion displayed in declaring, 'נַעֲשֶׂה וְנִשְׁמָע, *We will do and we will listen!' (Mechilta; Midrash Shemos Rabbah* 28:2, see *Yefeh Toar* and *Etz Yoseif;* see Overview).

The Midrash (*Shemos Rabbah* 29:9) emphasizes that when God spoke on this occasion the earth was silent without a sound to distort the sound of His words:

When the Holy One, Blessed be He, presented the Torah at Sinai not a bird chirped, not a fowl flew, not an ox lowed, not an angel ascended, not a seraph proclaimed *Kadosh* [*Holy*]. The sea did not roll and no creature made a sound. All of the vast universe was silent and mute. It was then that the Voice went forth and proclaimed: *'I* [*alone*] *am HASHEM, your God!'*

[The Jews had just been liberated from the idolatrous culture of Egypt where the forces of nature were worshiped as gods that controlled man's destiny. At Sinai, God silenced all of these natural forces in order to demonstrate that He alone controls every aspect of creation.]

Rashi notes that the Divine Name used here — Elohim — represents God in His role as the דַּיָּן, *Judge,* Who dispenses justice strictly, according to what each individual deserves, for good or ill. The use of this Name in the context of the Ten Commandments emphasizes the uncompromising manner with which God insists upon observance of these precepts. Whether or not one observes them is not left to the discretion of the individual Jew; they *must* be obeyed. In this respect, the Ten Commandments are different from many other *mitzvos,* which depend on circumstances or personal wishes. For example, one who does not live in his own or rented quarters is not required to put up a *mezuzah,* and one who has not sinned has no need to bring a sin offering. Anyone who fails to observe the Ten Commandments, however, must answer to God, the Judge.

אֵת כָּל־הַדְּבָרִים הָאֵלֶּה — *All these statements.*

This entire phrase seems su-

God spoke all these statements, saying:

² I am HASHEM, your God, Who delivered you

perfluous since it would have been sufficient for the verse to say וַיְדַבֵּר אֱלֹהִים לֵאמֹר, *And God spoke, saying* — and then go on to list the Ten Commandments (*Maharzu*).

Rashi (quoting *Mechilta*) comments that the presentation of the Ten Commandments began with a miracle that is incomprehensible in human terms: God uttered the entire Ten Commandments, *all these statements*, in a single utterance.

Gur Aryeh explains that the purpose of this single utterance was to symbolize to Israel that the entire Torah is a single, inseparable unit. The Ten Commandments and the Torah as a whole are not a collection of separate commandments and elements; they are one whole. Consequently, no one can say that he can abrogate or ignore one word or one commandment without affecting the remainder of the Torah. This is why the Sages teach that someone who denies the Divine origin of even a single word of the Torah has made a heretical statement.

The Midrash (*Shemos Rabbah* 28:4) explains that God said everything at once to demonstrate vividly that He is capable of performing any number of seemingly contradictory deeds at once, because He is the Omnipotent ruler and Controller of every force in creation. 'God simultaneously puts some to death and brings others to life. He smites one and cures another. Everyone in danger cries out to him — the mother in labor, the sailor in a storm, the traveler in the wilderness, the prisoner in his dungeon — one in the east, another in the west, one in the north, the

other in the south — all cry out at once and God hears each one's personal call.'

The Midrash goes on to say the extra word כָּל, *all*, has profound implications. *All* that God ever intended to communicate to mankind was uttered at Sinai. Every prophecy which the prophets were later to express was uttered at Sinai. Every law, every interpretation, every novel insight that was destined to be revealed and promulgated to mankind was originally uttered at Sinai.

Thus far we have described what God said; now we approach the question of what the Jewish people heard. This is a subject of controversy among the major commentators.

Expounding on the verse: תּוֹרָה צִוָּה-לָנוּ מֹשֶׁה, *Moses commanded us the Torah* (*Deuteronomy* 33:4) the Talmud (*Makkos* 24a) notes that the numerical value of the word תּוֹרָה, *Torah*, is 611 [ת = 400, ו = 6, ר = 200, ה = 5]. The verse may then be understood: *Moses commanded us 611 mitzvos*. With the addition of the first two commandments, which Israel heard directly from the mouth of the Almighty at Sinai, the total is 613.

Rashi explains that first all the commandments were uttered by God in a single instant. Then, God repeated the first two commandments word for word. Following that, the people were afraid that they could no longer endure the awesome holiness of God's voice and they asked that Moses repeat the remaining eight commandments to them. (*v.* 16).

According to *Rambam (Moreh Nevuchim* II: 32), the above passage indicates that Israel heard only the first two commandments from God, but they did not hear Him utter the other eight commandments at all. Even in the case of the first two commandments they did not hear the words clearly, but merely heard the sound. Thus in *Deuteronomy* 4:12 we read that Moses said, *You heard* קוֹל דְּבָרִים, *the sound of words,* i.e. the people heard a Heavenly sound, but could not distinguish any words.

Moses however, clearly heard all the words of the Ten Commandments; then he repeated and explained all that he had heard.

Rashi (v. 1) and *Ramban (v. 7)* have a different view. The simple reading of our verse indicates clearly that *God spoke 'all' these statements* [simultaneously] to the Jewish people, but there was a significant difference between the first two commandments and the others. Even though they were listening to the awesome pronouncements of God, Israel was granted the endurance and ability to comprehend the first two commandments because they are the fundamentals of the entire Jewish faith. Although they heard the other eight commandments with their own ears, they could neither distinguish nor comprehend the words. They were so awestruck that they could not understand what was being said. Consequently, Moses later repeated these eight commandments so that the people could know what they were.

Ramban points out that the first two commandments were said in first person, indicating that God was speaking directly to Israel. The other eight commandments, however, are in third person, implying that Moses related them to the Jews on God's behalf.

Moreover, *Meam Loez* observes, the first two commandments are contained in the same paragraph while each of the others is in a separate paragraph of its own. This, too, indicates the special manner in which the first two commandments were transmitted.

לֵאמֹר — *Saying.*

Throughout Scripture this word, as used when God Himself is speaking, introduces the direct quote, i.e., *saying* the following to the listener. Usually it also means that God is urging the listener to repeat His words to others.

R' Bachya differentiates between דִּבּוּר, *speech* and אֲמִירָה, *saying.* A דִּבּוּר is a statement dealing with the נִגְלָה, *revealed aspect* of Torah, the simple meaning. However, אֲמִירָה refers to the נִסְתָּר, *concealed,* esoteric message implied by the words. Thus God transmitted to Moses both the simple text of the Commandments and the secret, kabbalistic meaning.

Rashi (based on *Mechilta*) interprets לֵאמֹר as a reference to Israel's response to God's Commandments.

They responded eagerly and were in complete accord with everything God said. Whenever God commanded that something positive be done, the Jews responded, 'Yes!' And whenever God prohibited something the Jews continued their acceptance by responding, 'No!'

◆§ **First Commandment:**
   To Acknowledge HASHEM as the One Omnipotent God.

The most basic of all fundamentals and the pillar of all true knowledge is the belief that God is the Creator, Who is infinite, timeless, and all-powerful. The *mitzvah* to acknowledge and believe this is the essence of the First Commandment in which God proclaims His existence to Israel *(Rambam, Yesodei HaTorah 1:1)*.

In his listing of the 613 commandments, *Rambam* cites this verse as the basis of the first positive precept *(Sefer HaMitzvos)*: 'We are commanded to believe in God who is the Supreme Cause and the Creator of everything in existence.'

This belief is the very essence of Judaism, because no other commandments need be accepted without prior belief in the sovereignty of the Supreme Deity who issues the commands.

Mechilta uses a parable to illustrate the relationship between the first fundamental command and those which follow it: A king conquered a country and his attendants urged him to promulgate decrees to his new subjects. He refused, saying: 'No! When they have accepted my sovereignty I will issue decrees to them. For if they do not accept my sovereignty, why should they obey my decrees?' Similarly, God said to Israel: 'I am HASHEM your God; I am He whose sovereignty you accepted in Egypt.'

When the people responded, 'Yes, yes,' God continued: 'Just as you have accepted My sovereignty, so you must accept My decrees.'

This belief in God is also the first of *Rambam's* Thirteen Cardinal Principles of Faith *(Comm. to Mishnah, Sanhedrin, ch. 10)*.

2. אָנֹכִי ה' אֱלֹהֶיךָ — *I am HASHEM, your God.*

The more common word for *I* is אֲנִי, however, the term אָנֹכִי is used to emphasize exclusiveness — I, and I alone am God *(Malbim)*. I alone am the Prime Cause of all existence *(Sforno)*.

Rashi [from *Mechilta*] explains why God deemed it necessary to identify Himself as the One Omnipotent Ruler of the universe, a fact that presumably was well known to the people of Israel: God assumed various guises when He revealed Himself to His people. When He split the Sea and destroyed Pharaoh's army, He appeared as a mighty warrior in battle. When He gave the Torah He appeared as an elderly scholar full of tender mercy. This apparent duality gave the pagans an opportunity to claim the existence of a plurality of deities. Therefore, God considered it imperative to proclaim: 'I [alone] am HASHEM, your God. I alone was in Egypt. I alone was at the sea. I alone am at Sinai. It was I in the past, and it will be I in the future. It is I in This World and it will be I in the World to Come ... as the prophet *(Isaiah 44:6)* said, *So said HASHEM ... 'I am the first and I am the last.'*

Moreover, twenty-two thousand ministering angels accompanied God when He descended on Sinai, each of them endowed with an aspect of His divinity. It was essential for God to declare that all these legions of angels were neither His equals nor His partners, merely His escorts and servants *(Shemos Rabbah 29:2)*[1].

Pesikta D'Rav Kahana (12) explains that God's revelation at Sinai was given in such a manner that each Jew received it according to his own capacity. From suckling infant to the wisest adult, each Jew absorbed God's word with a different degree of sophistication. Upon

1. *Midrash Tanchuma Yashan* relates that when God began creation with the word בְּרֵאשִׁית [*in the beginning*] that starts with the letter ב, *beis*, the letter א, *aleph*, protested: 'I am the first

comparing their differing perceptions, the people could conclude that a thousand different gods had spoken. To avoid such a misapprehension, God introduced His revelation by, declaring, אָנֹכִי ה' אֱלֹהֶיךָ, I [alone] am HASHEM, your God [see Rashi to Psalms 29:4 and Shemos Rabbah 5:9, 29:1, 34:1].

ה' אֱלֹהֶיךָ — HASHEM, your God.

'Just as you have accepted me as your God, I shall always be directly accessible to your prayers. Therefore, pray to Me alone and serve Me alone; no intermediaries are necessary' (Sforno).

In all the commandments, God addressed Israel in the second person singular form as if He were speaking to only one individual. Therefore He said, 'I am HASHEM [אֱלֹהֶיךָ] your God,' using the singular possessive suffix ךָ, cha, instead of the plural suffix כֶם, chem.

This usage teaches every Jew to feel: 'The Ten Commandments and the entire Torah were addressed directly to me; I personally am responsible for the Torah and I cannot excuse myself by saying it is enough if others observe the commandments.' Each individual must feel as if he is alone in the world and that the very existence of the universe is dependent exclusively on his own Torah study and observance. Moreover, he must realize that it is not sufficient to be a practicing Jew only when he is in the company of others who observe him and encourage him; he must be self-reliant (Meam Loez).

Rashi offers another reason for the use of the singular form אֱלֹהֶיךָ your God. It was God's intention to provide Moses with an argument to defend Israel's sin of worshiping the golden calf: since the commandment was expressed in the singular, the people could have thought that God was speaking to only one person — Moses. Indeed, when God expressed the intention to destroy Israel for having made the idol, Moses protested, 'Why O God are You wrathful against Your people (Exodus 32:11). Israel cannot be condemned for making another god, because You, O Lord, gave them grounds for error! Since You proclaimed the Ten Commandments in the singular, the Jews thought that the commandments were addressed only to me! Furthermore, O Lord, You proclaimed, You [singular] shall have no other gods; so, again, the Jews were misled into thinking that only I [Moses] was forbidden to fashion an idol.'

אֲשֶׁר הוֹצֵאתִיךָ מֵאֶרֶץ מִצְרַיִם — Who

letter of the Hebrew alphabet so it is only right that the creation of the world should begin with me!'

God comforted the aleph: 'Fear not, the holy Torah preceded the world, and when I present it to Israel I will begin My revelation with anochi [אָנֹכִי], a word that begins with an aleph.'

R' Yaakov Moshe Charlop explains this dialogue homiletically. The aleph argued that because it stands for 'oneness' and 'unity', symbolizing consistency and harmony — it is the most appropriate letter with which to keynote creation. The Holy One, Blessed be He, had a different thought, however. Better that the world should be created with the letter beis, the numerical equivalent of two. 'Two' represents plurality, diversity, contrast — even conflict. This is essential to the success of God's plan — to establish a world full of challenge and opposition, so that man can strive to bring harmony and purpose to the diverse elements of the universe. Such harmony can be achieved through the commandments of the Torah — and they are introduced with aleph, the letter of unity and oneness.

from the land of Egypt, from the house of slavery.

delivered you from the land of Egypt.

Ibn Ezra and *Chizkuni* discuss why God based His authority on the Exodus instead of identifying Himself as the Creator of heaven and earth. God wished to establish the justice of giving more commandments and responsibilities to Israel than to any other nation. God has done more for Israel than for any other nation; never before nor since has an entire nation been removed from the bowels of an oppressive nation after centuries of exile and bondage.

Thus, this very first command teaches the importance of gratitude, for God based His claim to our allegiance on the favors He did for us. *Rashi* comments: God's miraculous deliverance of Israel from Egypt is sufficient reason for us to subject ourselves to Him.

We find in *Mishnas R' Eliezer*: The ingrate who denies the good that is done him is considered as if he denies the existence of God, because our belief in God is based upon our gratitude for His goodness to us.

R' Bachya gives a different explanation for God's mention of the Exodus, and not Creation. Before giving the Commandments, God wished to establish His sovereignty by means of proof that all the Jews had seen with their own eyes. No human eye had witnessed the wonders of Creation, but hundreds of thousands of Jews had witnessed their salvation from Egypt a scant seven weeks before the revelation at Sinai. Indeed, God's miracles during the period of the plagues demonstrated vividly how completely He controls every aspect of nature

and bore testimony to His creation of every molecule of the universe.

R' Yonah offers yet another explanation: God said to Israel: 'My children, there are times when My commands will seem harsh and incomprehensible, but I ask you to trust that I mean your benefit. Did I not redeem you from Egypt for your own sake? So too, you may be certain that everything I ask you to do is not for My sake, but for yours!'

The *Zohar* discusses why the Torah constantly reminds us of the redemption from Egypt, and even begins the Ten Commandments with it. God did much more than merely release Israel from physical bondage. Israel had been corrupted by the immoral environment of Egypt. It had fallen to the forty-ninth level of spiritual contamination [מ״ט שַׁעֲרֵי טֻמְאָה]. Had it descended to the fiftieth — and lowest — level of impurity, Israel would have been beyond redemption. When God liberated the Jews, He also freed their souls from the corrupt influence of Egypt and the Evil Inclination. He allowed them to shed the baseness of Egypt and to ascend fifty levels of purity and perception of truth.

To recall this spiritual ascent, we count the forty-nine days from the second day of Pesach to Shavuos. These forty-nine days between redemption and revelation correspond to the forty-nine levels of impurity. Each day God raised Israel from one level of defilement and allowed the people to gain one new level of sanctity. On the fiftieth day, Shavuos, they attained the heights of purity and the Torah was given.

ג לֹא־יִהְיֶה לְךָ אֱלֹהִים אֲחֵרִים עַל־פָּנָי:

מִבֵּית עֲבָדִים — *From the house of slavery* [lit. *slaves*].

The Egyptians were among the descendants of Ham *(Genesis 10:6)*, the lowliest of peoples; indeed, our verse describes Egypt as a *house of slaves*. Israel, on the other hand, was an aristocratic nation, a kingdom of priests *(Exodus 19:6)*. Thus, it was especially degrading for Israel to be enslaved by Egypt; it is bad enough to be the slave of a noble, but there is nothing more humiliating than for an aristocrat to be the servant of a slave *(R' Bachya)*.

[Furthermore, Egypt was like a fortified prison camp. It was so well guarded that no slave could escape alive. Thus, the term *house of slavery* is an apt description of the walls and ramparts that imprisoned the hopeless slaves.]

⊷§ Second Commandment:
Prohibition against all aspects of idol worship

[The Second Commandment spans four verses and contains four separate negative precepts, all prohibiting various aspects of idolatry.]

3. לֹא־יִהְיֶה לְךָ אֱלֹהִים אֲחֵרִים — *You shall not recognize* [lit. *there shall not be to you*] *the gods of others.*

Sefer HaChinuch explains: We may not believe in any god other than HASHEM ... This precept is the great principle upon which the entire Torah depends, for our Sages said *(Sifri, Bamidbar 111)*: Whoever accepts the idols as deities is considered to have denied the entire Torah. One is in violation of this commandment if he: declares his acceptance of any god other than the Almighty; worships a false deity in its *own* customary manner of service, even if that particular service would not be considered a form of worship under Torah law; or venerates it through one of four ways that Torah law designates as universal forms of worship. These four modes of service are: slaughtering a sacrifice; burning the flesh of such an offering; pouring a libation [or blood *(Sanhedrin* 60b)] before it; or prostrating oneself before it.

Rashi (based on *Mechilta)* warns that we should not translate the term אֱלֹהִים אֲחֵרִים as *other gods,* which imply that there *are* gods other than the Almighty, albeit inferior to Him. Rather, stresses *Rashi,* the proper translation of the phrase is *gods of others* [i.e., *other nations*]. Thus Israel is warned not to give credence to the gods of the pagan nations.

Alternatively, *Rashi* renders the term אֱלֹהִים אֲחֵרִים as *stranger-like gods,* because the idols are like strangers toward their worshipers. When idolators are imperiled, they pray fervently to their gods — but there is no response; the gods are like total strangers who show no recognition to those who appeal to them.

Rambam, on the other hand, gives a spiritual connotation to the term. It refers to the angels whom God designated as guardians of individual nations or the angels who carry out God's will in the functioning of nature. In time, people begin to think that these celestial beings — which were God-like in the sense that they were spiritual and incorporeal — were gods.

³ You shall not recognize the gods of others before My presence. ⁴ You shall not make yourself a carved

Mechilta translates אֱלֹהִים אֲחֵרִים as *different gods*, because idolators constantly change the images they worship. First they make an idol of gold, but when they find themselves short of money they melt down the golden 'god' and replace it with a statue of silver. If they need more money, they melt down the silver god and replace it with a copper figure, and so it goes. The Torah scornfully describes this process of incessant change (*Deuteronomy* 32:17): *New gods which appeared only recently, which your fathers feared not.*

Rambam (*Yesodei HaTorah* 1:6) rules: We may not even consider the possibility that there is any deity other than HASHEM, the One and Only God. Whoever entertains such a thought is considered as denying the basic principle of the Jewish faith, the tenet upon which our entire religion is based.

R' Bachya adds that we must attribute all power to God alone, and not accept the sovereignty of any angel, star or constellation, even though God assigns to such celestial forces a measure of control over the fortunes of mankind. These forces have no power of their own, however. [Following this interpretation, *R' Bachya* renders אֱלֹהִים not as *gods*, but as *powers*. The word אֱלֹהִים is frequently used in connection with those who possess authority, such as angels, courts, and rulers.] Accordingly our verse would be rendered *powers* [whose authority derives from] *another source*, i.e., HASHEM, Who grants them the power to exert a measure

of influence over the world.

Thus, *Isaiah* declares in the name of God, אֲנִי רִאשׁוֹן וַאֲנִי אַחֲרוֹן וּמִבַּלְעָדַי אֵין אֱלֹהִים, *I am the first and I am the last and beside Me there is no god* (*Isaiah* 44:6), i.e., I do not derive My strength from any other deity, rather I alone am the Source of all power.

עַל־פָּנָי — *Before My presence* [lit. *My face*].

I.e. for as long as I live — forever — and wherever I am — the entire universe. The injunction against idolatry was not limited to the era or region of the people who stood at Sinai, but to all generations wherever they may be (*Mechilta; Rashi*).

I am Omnipresent; wherever idolatry is practiced, it is *before My presence* (*Ibn Ezra; Sforno*). *Ibn Ezra* quotes a wise man who paraphrased this warning: 'O servant! do not brazenly anger your Master while he is watching — and God is always watching!'

Even if a person believes in the *presence* — the all-powerful sovereignty — of God, but persists in the belief that there exists another deity of equal stature, he is violating this commandment.

Midrash Asseres HaDibros records that God said to Israel: No matter what kind of *face*, i.e. attitude, I display towards you, do not abandon Me. At times I must show you a countenance of anger or vengeance in order to force you to mend your ways. Do not be affronted and seek to spite Me by taking a different god because you are displeased by *My face*, in its current manifestation.

ד לֹא־תַעֲשֶׂה לְךָ פֶסֶל וְכָל־תְּמוּנָה אֲשֶׁר
בַּשָּׁמַיִם מִמַּעַל וַאֲשֶׁר בָּאָרֶץ מִתָּחַת
ה וַאֲשֶׁר בַּמַּיִם מִתַּחַת לָאָרֶץ: לֹא־

4. לֹא־תַעֲשֶׂה לְךָ פֶסֶל — *You shall not make yourself a carved image.*

The term פֶסֶל usually refers to a sculpture, generally something carved from wood or stone. However, it can also refer to any three-dimensional image, no matter how it is produced. In the context of our verse, the material from which, or the method by which, the image is made would make no difference (R' Hirsch).

[This verse adds to the prohibition of the previous one. Whereas earlier the Torah had forbidden the worship of existing beings or idols, depending on the various interpretations cited above, here the Torah speaks of an attempt to fashion an image or likeness that would then be worshiped.]

Sefer HaChinuch cites *Rambam* (Hilchos Avodah Zarah 3:9): One may not make images to be worshiped — even if the one who makes the image does not worship it himself. The very act of manufacturing idols is forbidden, in order to keep such 'stumbling-blocks' to our belief far removed from us. It makes no difference whether one manufactures the image with his own hands or orders it made [by someone else]; even if one merely causes such an image to be produced he transgresses the precept of *You shall not make yourself a carved image or any likeness.*

Ramban disagrees, maintaining that this verse prohibits only the manufacture of idols for personal worship. The prohibition against making idols for others is given in *Exodus* 20:23 and *Leviticus* 26:1.

The Talmud (*Sanhedrin* 61a) infers from our verse that someone who declares himself to be a god and succeeds in persuading others to worship him is liable to the death penalty, for it says *You shall not make 'yourself'* [לְךָ] *an idol.*

Mechilta d'Rashbi identifies פֶסֶל as cognate with פָּסוּל, *defective, unfit, rejected.* God warned: He who makes idols rejects Me; let him beware, for I will reject *him* from the world.

Ohr HaChaim uses a similar interpretation to explain why some idols are called *elohim* [gods] (v. 3) and others are called carved images, as in our verse. *Rambam (Hil. Avodah Zarah* ch. 1) describes the historical development of idolatry. The earliest generations of mankind recognized that God was the Creator, but in time, people began to preach that man should honor God's servants — sun, stars, the power of vegetation and so on — much as one honors a king by showing respect for his ministers. This was bad enough, but the transgression was compounded when later generations began to insist that the 'ministers' themselves were gods. Thus, we find two categories of 'gods': one that is regarded as a true deity and another that is important only because it is the servant of a deity. The second sort of god can be disregarded or replaced, as circumstances warrant.

image nor any likeness of that which is in the heavens above, or on the earth below, or in the water beneath the earth. **⁵** *You shall not prostrate yourself*

For example, a river may be worshiped as the source of irrigation and fertility, but if it runs dry, it will be discarded in favor of some other body of water. This sort of god is called פֶּסֶל from the word פָּסוּל, *defective*, for a god that is served only as a convenience, is inherently 'defective.'

וְכָל־תְּמוּנָה — *Nor any likeness.*

In contrast to פֶּסֶל, which is a relatively accurate three-dimensional image of something or other, תְּמוּנָה, *likeness* is a symbolic representation or picture (*R' Hirsch*). As *Chizkuni* explains one may wish to worship God, but feel that he must channel his devotion toward something tangible. Therefore he may choose to create a form that will symbolize the object of his loyalty.[1]

אֲשֶׁר בַּשָּׁמַיִם מִמַּעַל וַאֲשֶׁר בָּאָרֶץ מִתָּחַת — *[Of] that [which is] in the heavens above, or on the earth below.*

The likeness spoken of above is a graphic portrayal intended to be similar to something that is seen in the heavens [or on earth] (*Rashi* as explained by *Gur Aryeh*).

Ramban explains that in ancient times people began to worship the sun, the moon, and the constellations, thinking that such worship would increase the power of the stars which, in turn, would bestow new strength on the worshipers. They would carve images or make likenesses of the heavenly bodies. In the case of constellations, they would make images of the figures formed by the stars, such as an archer, scorpion, or lion.

Closely related to this form of idolatry was the worship of human beings. Sometimes people noticed that someone had great power and that he was uncommonly successful. The masses attributed this to his spiritual power and felt that if they acknowledged his supremacy by deifying him, their fortunes would ascend with his. Such was the case with Pharaoh, Sennacherib and Nebuchadnezzar, who declared themselves to be gods, worthy of veneration and worship, and set up statues or likenesses of themselves.

The Talmud (*Rosh Hashanah* 24b) teaches that the words *on the earth* include a prohibition against deifying geographic points such as mountains and hills, seas, rivers, and valleys. The final word מִתָּחַת, *below*, alludes to even the tiniest worm that burrows beneath the earth's surface.

וַאֲשֶׁר בַּמַּיִם מִתַּחַת לָאָרֶץ — *Or in the water beneath the earth.*

In its simple meaning, this stich forbids the fashioning of images of undersea creatures. *Ramban* comments that it refers to the form of idolatry in which people began venerating evil spiritual forces known as שֵׁדִים, *demons*. Some such forces have the power to harm man

1. *Baal HaTurim* (*Deuteronomy* 5:8) notes that the *vav* of וְכָל has the numerical value of six, which alludes to six major categories of likenesses — male, female, animal, fowl, reptile and fish — all of which are enumerated in *Deuteronomy* 4:16-18, where the Torah re-emphasizes its warning against idolatry.

תִּשְׁתַּחֲוֶה לָהֶם וְלֹא תָעָבְדֵם כִּי אָנֹכִי יְהוָה אֱלֹהֶיךָ אֵל קַנָּא פֹּקֵד עֲוֹן אָבֹת

and they could be harnessed by the magicians and false prophets of Scriptural times. [The magicians of Pharaoh, for example, were able to duplicate the first two plagues because they possessed the now-lost art of utilizing these evil powers.] Scripture ridicules Jews who believe in demonolatry, saying (*Deuteronomy* 32:17): *They sacrificed to demons, non-gods, gods that they knew not, new gods that came up of late which your fathers feared not.* Our verse describes them as being *in the water beneath the earth* because they would conceal themselves there.

5. לֹא־תִשְׁתַּחֲוֶה לָהֶם — *You shall not prostrate yourself to them.*

Sefer HaChinuch explains: One may not prostrate himself before the idols with the intention of worshiping them. Prostration means lying flat with the hands and feet on the ground or touching the face to the ground before the idol. This is one of the four universal modes of worship — the others being sacrifice of animals, burning their flesh and libation of wine or other liquids. Even if this particular idol is not usually worshiped in one of these four ways, anyone who serves him in this manner incurs guilt through this action.

The Talmud (*Avodah Zarah* 12a) teaches that it is improper to do anything vaguely resembling prostration before an idol. Thus, if a thorn lodged in a person's foot or his money was scattered before an idol, he is not allowed to remove the thorn or to gather the coins in such a way that it appears to be bowing toward the idol.

The Talmud (*Sanhedrin* 61a) says that it is forbidden to bow to a man who proclaims himself a god. It *is* permissible, however, to bow to someone like a king or holy man out of fear or honor.

וְלֹא תָעָבְדֵם — *Nor worship them.*

Sefer HaChinuch writes: We may not worship any idol in the usual manner of those who believe in it, even if their customary method of service is *not* one of the four primary forms enumerated above. A person incurs the death penalty even if he worships the idol in a seemingly degrading manner, provided idolators normally worship the idol in such a fashion. For example, the idolators would defecate in front of Pe'or, they would throw stones at Merkulis [Mercury] or bring hair as an offering to Chemosh. [But if, for example, someone threw stones at Pe'or or defecated in front of Merkulis, he would not be in violation because these would be obvious expressions of contempt.]

[Thus, in the verses comprised by the Second Commandment, we find four negative commandments:

(A) not to believe in idols;

(B) not to make idols;

(C) not to worship them by means of the four universal modes of service;

(D) not to worship them by the means of their own particular religions.]

כִּי אָנֹכִי ה' אֱלֹהֶיךָ אֵל קַנָּא — *For I [am]* HASHEM, *your God — a jealous God.*

R' Bachya explains: אָנֹכִי, *I, alone,*

to them nor worship them; for I am HASHEM, your
God — a jealous God, remembering the sins of fathers

am HASHEM, your God, and you may not abandon Me for some other false deity. If you dare to betray Me, remember, I am אֵל קַנָּא, a jealous God, Who has awesome powers of retribution. [1]

Nowhere in Scripture is God's anger against Israel described with the term 'jealousy' except with regard to idol worship. This idea is emphasized by the Mechilta: God says, 'For idolatry I zealously exact punishment, but in other matters, I am gracious and merciful.'

Ramban explains the reason for this. Israel accepted God's sovereignty at Sinai and, in return, was designated as His chosen nation. This intimate relationship resembles the bond of matrimony between a man and wife. A Jew who worships another god is like a spouse willfully engaging in adultery; the betrayed partner — God — is justified in His anger.

[Although the expression קַנָּא, jealous, is used against Israel only

when idolatry is involved, it is used against non-Jewish nations when God promises to punish them for their crimes against Israel. The reasoning is similar: because the nations have wronged God's 'spouse,' He will avenge Himself against them.]

R' Hirsch relates קַנָּא, jealous, to the similar word קָנָה, owning. Thus the concept of justifiable jealousy is that someone with a claim to the allegiance or benefit of a person or thing need not permit it to be illegally claimed by someone else. Since only God has the right to the dedication and worship of the Jew — He is the Owner, as it were — He will not permit this service to be diverted to an idol.

Therefore, Scripture contains no account of a prophet chastising any other nation for idolatry. Israel alone is rebuked for such a betrayal, as it is written (Deuteronomy 4:20): [Only] you did HASHEM take for Himself (Ramban; R' Bachya).

1. A non-Jewish philosopher asked Rabban Gamliel: 'It is written in your Torah, "I am HASHEM, your God, a jealous God:" is there anything to these false idols that makes them worthy of Divine jealousy? A warrior is jealous of another warrior. A scholar is jealous of another scholar. A rich man is jealous of another rich man. But why should God be jealous of worthless idols?'

Rabban Gamliel replied: 'This divine jealousy can be compared to a husband who marries a second wife in addition to his first spouse. If the second wife is superior to the first in every way, then the first wife has no legitimate cause for jealousy. But if the second wife is inferior, the first wife will be infuriated.'

Another philosopher asked Rabban Gamliel: 'Sometimes events seem to indicate that God does recognize the powers of the idol, for it may happen that an entire city burns down with the exception of the pagan temple.'

Rabban Gamliel replied: 'This can be illustrated with the example of a king who went out to war. With whom does he battle — with the living or with the dead? Of course, only with the living, there is no need to attack the dead. Similarly God does not punish the idols, because they are dead and powerless.'

Again, the philosoper asked Rabban Gamliel: 'In the final analysis the idols are worthless; they serve only as a stumbling-block to lead people astray. Why doesn't God sweep these idols from the earth once and for all?'

Rabban Gamliel replied: 'Do they worship only idols? They also worship the sun, the moon, the stars and the constellations; the mountains, hills, springs and valleys; they even worship their fellowmen! Should God destroy His entire creation because of these fools?' (Mechilta).

עַל־בָּנִים עַל־שִׁלֵּשִׁים וְעַל־רִבֵּעִים
לְשֹׂנְאָי: וְעֹשֶׂה חֶסֶד לַאֲלָפִים לְאֹהֲבַי ו

◆§ Punishment on Future Generations

The verse now goes on to say that the punishment of idolators may be deferred to future offspring, up to the fourth generation. The difficulty of this concept is raised by the Talmud (Sanhedrin 27b): Since the Torah itself lays down the dictum that: *Fathers shall not die for sons nor shall sons die for fathers; a man shall die only for his own sins* (Deuteronomy 24:16), how can the Torah contradict itself and say, as our verse does, that punishment is inflicted on future generations? The Talmud replies that offspring are punished only if the children grasp the sins of their forefathers as their 'own' or 'if it was in the power of the children to protest but they failed to do so.'

The key to both explanations is that children share the responsibility — and hence deserve the punishment — only if they adopt the sins as their own. They can do this by adopting the sinful ways of their forefathers even though they recognize them as evil, or if they permit the original sins to take place despite having the ability to prevent them. If they share in the complicity of the sins, then two, three, or four generations may be considered partners in the transgression.

A further concept is set forth here by the major commentators. In the Divine scheme, God is patient with sinners until they overstep their bounds. Were He to punish people or nations as soon as they transgressed, no man could survive His justified wrath. But that is not God's way. Instead, He ordains in His wisdom that He will hold back His retribution so that the sinner can have the opportunity to repent, or so that children can be better, or so that some good may yet come of the person or family. God also sets a limit beyond which He will not allow sins to continue to accumulate. Until that limit is reached, לֹא נִתְמַלְאָה סְאָתָם, *their measure [of sin] has not been filled*, and He may withhold punishment. Once נִתְמַלְאָה סְאָתָם, *their measure has been filled*, He waits no longer. So it is that God told Abraham that the Canaanites would not be required to give up *Eretz Yisrael* for over four hundred years, because their quota of sin had not been filled (Genesis 15:16, see ArtScroll comm.). In the case of a family, our verse tells us that God may let sins go unpunished for up to four generations. The growing accumulation of sin is carried forward from generation to generation, but never is anyone punished for more than four generations of sin even if, as described above, he is complicitous. If, however, the 'measure is filled' in the second, third, or fourth generation, the total punishment may be inflicted at that point.

In no case, are *innocent* offspring punished for sins of parents. And even this doctrine of punishment carried over to later generations was later annulled. (See footnote below, s.v. לְשֹׂנְאָי.)

פֹּקֵד עֲוֹן אָבֹת עַל־בָּנִים — *Remembering the sins of fathers upon children.*
Although He does not punish immediately, He does not forget the sins that merit punishment; He merely delays the punishment, but does not forgo it. In this view, the verse is continuing the theme of God's unforgiving wrath against idolators. The delay should not be interpreted as a lack of knowledge or will (Rambam).

Ibn Ezra, however, interprets this as an expression of mercy. Instead of punishing immediately, God remembers what was done, but defers retribution in the interest of allowing the sinner or his children to repent (Ibn Ezra).

Ohr HaChaim, in an interpretation similar to *Ibn Ezra's,* explains the juxtaposition of this phrase, describing God's merciful patience, with the earlier one that describes God as *jealous* and unforgiving of idol worship. It is true, we are informed, that God is *jealous;* if so, one may wonder why it is that so many sinners walk the earth serenely? The verse answers that God defers punishment for up to four generations to allow time for repentance. Otherwise, no human being could survive.

עַל־שִׁלֵּשִׁים וְעַל־רִבֵּעִים — *To* [lit. *upon*] *the third and fourth* [*generations*].

God will wait from generation to generation until the measure is filled *(Ramban).*

He will delay punishment even for sinners until the fourth generation. By then, if there has been no repentance, the evil is too strongly entrenched to be uprooted, and the punishment will come *(Ibn Ezra; Ohr HaChaim).*

Sforno, in a novel interpretation, differentiates between the third and fourth generations. The third generation will be punished if it is worse than earlier ones. The fourth generation, however, will be punished even if it only maintains the

earlier traditions of family sinfulness, for after so many generations the hope for repentance has evaporated.

לְשׂנְאָי — *Of My enemies.*

This is the key word in explaining why grown children should be punished for the sins of their parents and grandparents. By adopting or approving the sins of their parents, as explained above, they stamp themselves as God's *enemies* and are deserving of His retribution.

Indeed, *R' Bachya* comments that the Torah expresses this concept in terms of four generations because it is common for that many generations of a family to be alive at the same time, with the youngest generation observing the bad examples of grandparents and great-grandparents. The great-grandchild may then be judged as having opted for the ways of his father, grandfather, and great-grandfather.[1]

6. וְעָשֶׂה חֶסֶד לַאֲלָפִים — *But showing kindness for thousands of generations.*

This verse teaches that the measure of Divine recompense for a good deed is five hundred times greater than the measure of Divine

1. *R' Moshe Eisemann* comments that this doctrine should not be understood simply to mean that children will be punished for their parents' guilt, given the proper circumstances. In the Torah the doctrine is stated in conjunction with the associated idea (v. 6) of God *showing kindness for thousands* [of generations]. That doctrine does *not* assert that the reward earned by the righteous man is given instead to his children, but that *part of his reward* is that God will be kind to his descendants. So, too, the wicked man is punished *partly* in that God will withhold His kindness from his descendants. The kindness and favors which God shows to every individual in helping him in his struggle for sanctity and goodness will be withheld from someone who obdurately clings to the evil ways of his father, thereby allowing him to cultivate unhindered his own propensity towards evil.

Makkos 24a cites the verse: הַנֶּפֶשׁ הַחֹטֵאת הִיא תָמוּת, *Whichever soul sins, it shall die* (*Ezekiel* 18:4). The Talmud concludes that Ezekiel 'annulled' the doctrine of Moses. Yet it is

ז וּלְשֹׁמְרֵי מִצְוֹתָי: לֹא תִשָּׂא
אֶת־שֵׁם־יהוה אֱלֹהֶיךָ לַשָּׁוְא כִּי לֹא

retribution for a sinful one. Concerning retribution, the preceding verse says that it can extend as much as four generations, while the reward for good carries over to at least two thousand generations [the minimum amount in 'thousands' of generations], which is five hundred times four (Tosefta Sotah 3:4).

Even to those who hate Him [v. 5], God is prepared to show kindness if they will but perform a good deed (Bereishis Rabbasi, Vayechi).

וּלְשֹׁמְרֵי מִצְוֹתָי לְאֹהֲבַי — To those who love Me and keep My commandments.

R' Shimon ben Elazar taught: One who serves God out of love far surpasses the one who serves Him out of fear. Scripture states here, that the merit of those who keep the commandments out of love endures for two thousand generations; however, in Deuteronomy 7:9, we read that those who keep the commandments out of fear are rewarded merely לְאֶלֶף דּוֹר, for one thousand generations (Sotah 31a).

Ramban defines those who love Me as the martyrs who joyfully sacrifice their lives for the sake of God's glory. They acknowledge no deity but the Almighty, and refuse

to worship idols even upon threat of death. Of such people, the Torah says: And you shall love HASHEM your God with all your heart, and with all your soul (Deuteronomy 6:15).

Because Abraham risked his life by refusing to worship the idols in the city of Ur of the Chaldees, the Prophet (Isaiah 41:8) singles him out saying, Abraham, the one who loves Me. Men of lesser devotion are called those who keep My commandments.

⊷§ Third Commandment:
Prohibition against vain oaths

7. לֹא תִשָּׂא אֶת־שֵׁם־ה' אֱלֹהֶיךָ לַשָּׁוְא — You shall not take [lit. carry] the Name of HASHEM, your God, in a vain oath.

[The prohibition refers not simply to mentioning God's Name in vain, but to swearing vainly by His Name. Nor does it refer to swearing falsely for profit or some other benefit; that is prohibited by Leviticus 19:12. Rather, our verse prohibits oaths, using God's Name, that serve no purpose, as is explained below.] Sefer HaChinuch lists four major categories of vain oaths:

difficult to understand how a doctrine given in the Torah could be described as the personal philosophy of Moses subject to annulment by a later prophet.

Maharal in Makkos suggests that Moses was the ideal אִישׁ הָאֱלֹהִים, Man of God [אֱלֹהִים denoting God as Judge], whose world-view demanded absolute and uncompromising justice. Moses' frame of reference was perfection; within that high standard, the shortcomings of parents might be deemed grievous enough to affect succeeding generations who continued in the well-trodden path of sin. However, Moses himself was aware that other leaders would arise in Israel, whose lesser degree of perfection would demand a more flexible and compromising mode of justice, according to which Moses' doctrine would be 'annulled.' Both concepts are part of God's plan: His wisdom decrees that sometimes He judge strictly and other times mercifully. What the Talmud describes as the doctrines of Moses and Ezekiel are nothing more than the familiar manifestations of judgment and mercy.

For a lengthy discussion of these concepts, see the ArtScroll Ezekiel 18:2-4.

of generations to those who love Me and keep My commandments.

⁷ You shall not take the Name of HASHEM, your God, in a vain oath; for HASHEM will not absolve

(A) swearing to contradict a clearly known fact, for example, that a marble pillar is made of gold;

(B) swearing to verify what is clearly known, for instance, that a clearly visible stone is a stone;

(C) swearing to violate any of God's commandments; such an oath serves no purpose, because man has no power to nullify what God has bound him to do [— since at Sinai, the entire nation of Israel swore to keep the commandments of the Torah with an oath that can never be cancelled, if one vows not to wear *tefillin* or *tzitzis*, or not to eat *matzah* or anything similar, it is considered a vain oath]; and

(D) swearing to do something that one obviously lacks the strength or ability to accomplish, for example, swearing not to sleep for three days in a row, or not to eat for seven days in a row [— since these feats are not humanly possible, the vow to accomplish them is worthless].

Sefer HaChinuch concludes: The purpose of this prohibition is to fortify our faith that there is none as mighty and enduring as the Holy One, Blessed be He. It is fitting therefore, that we mention His Name with awe and fear, quivering and trembling — not like the revelers who speak of trivial matters whose existence is temporary and are soon lost to oblivion.

Seder Eliyahu Rabbah 24 derives a relationship between the first three commandments. Someone who utters God's Name in vain is considered as evil as an idol worshiper, while someone who is careful *not* to utter God's Name for naught gives honor and pleasure to the Creator Who said, *'I alone am HASHEM your God.'* [Idolatry is possible only if one denies the greatness of God, and one who stands in proper awe of God could never pay homage to a stranger's god. Similarly, one with a proper reverence for God's Name would never use it frivolously in an oath.]

Ramban points out that Scripture does not use the phrase לֹא תִשָּׁבַע, *you shall not swear*, instead it says לֹא תִשָּׂא, *You shall not 'take' God's Name in vain*. This is meant to imply that it is forbidden to mention God's Name unnecessarily at any time, even *without* an oath. The Rabbis call this מוֹצִיא שֵׁם שָׁמַיִם לְבַטָּלָה, *uttering the Name of Heaven uselessly* (Temurah 3b; Nedarim 10b).

The Talmud (*Berachos* 33a) teaches that whoever recites God's Name in an unnecessary blessing transgresses the command, *You shall not take the Name ... in vain.* Furthermore, poverty [and tragedy] is to be found only in a home where God's Name is mentioned in vain (*She'iltos, Yisro*).

Pesikta Rabbasi 22 offers a number of homiletical interpretations of this verse. It renders: *Do not carry HASHEM's Name upon yourself,* i.e., don't set yourself up as God's representative and a Torah authority if you are not worthy of such a mantle.

יְנַקֶּה יהוה אֵת אֲשֶׁר־יִשָּׂא אֶת־שְׁמוֹ
לַשָּׁוְא:
ח־ט זָכוֹר אֶת־יוֹם הַשַּׁבָּת לְקַדְּשׁוֹ: שֵׁשֶׁת

Also, do not wear holy articles to look like a man of God and then, disregarding His Name, go forth and commit transgressions.[1]

כִּי לֹא יְנַקֶּה ה' אֵת אֲשֶׁר־יִשָּׂא אֶת־שְׁמוֹ לַשָּׁוְא — For HASHEM will not absolve anyone who takes His Name in a vain oath.

This phrase implies that an atonement sufficient for other sins cannot bring forgiveness for the transgression of swearing vainly. The Torah takes pains to spell this out — HASHEM will not absolve — because people tend to feel that oaths can be taken lightly.

Ibn Ezra explains that an oath, by definition, means that a person declares, 'My word is as true as is God Himself!' If his word is false or his oath is taken frivolously, he has indicated contempt for God, ח"ו — clearly a grievous sin.

Rambam (Hilchos Shavuos 12:1) writes: Even though the person who swears in vain has been punished [by the Beis Din], the sin of his oath has not been fully atoned for, because it says, HASHEM will not absolve. This person has no acquittal from the heavenly judgment until he has been punished for having desecrated the Great Name ... Therefore, a person must beware of this sin more than all other sins.

The Talmud (Shabbos 33a) teaches that in retribution for vain oaths, many catastrophes can occur, such as violent attacks by an enemy who plunders property, plagues, famine, and attack by wild beasts who lose their natural fear of men.

The Midrash (Bamidbar Rabbah, Mattos) relates that King Alexander Yannai, a member of the Hasmonean dynasty, suffered the destruction of two thousand cities because he was prone to swear excessively, even though he never swore falsely and always carried out his oaths. Nevertheless, he was punished for making unnecessary oaths.

The Talmud (Gittin 35a) tells of a woman who was negligent in the care of someone else's money. Not knowing where it was, she swore that she had not used the money, and invoked heavenly punishment upon herself if she had done so. She indeed suffered a personal tragedy, even though she thought she was being truthful. When the Rabbis learned of what happened they said, 'This woman thought she was swearing truthfully, and still she was punished. Someone who knowingly swears falsely will surely be punished.'

Tosefta (Sotah 7) and the Talmud (Shavuos 39a) state: When a man must take an oath the court issues a

1. Pesikta Rabbasi elaborates on this theme: In ancient times, most Jews wore their tefillin all day long, but they stopped this practice because of the hypocrites who misrepresented themselves by wearing tefillin. This was illustrated by the unfortunate experience of a certain man who was carrying his money on a Friday. Toward sunset, he went to a synagogue where he found someone wearing tefillin and praying. Some say this person was a false proselyte. The man carrying the money said to himself, 'Should I not feel safe to leave my money with this person who [even at this late hour in the day] wears the proof of his fear of God?' Thereupon he left his money with that person. But at the end of the Sabbath, when he came

anyone who takes His Name in a vain oath.
8 Remember the Sabbath day to sanctify it. 9 Six

warning in the severest terms possible: Be aware that the entire world shook and trembled at the moment the Almighty said at Sinai, '*You shall not take the Name of HASHEM your God, in a vain oath.*' Concerning other sins mentioned in Scripture the Torah says that God will forgive and absolve the sinner. Only here does it say, *HASHEM will not absolve.* Concerning all sins only the sinner himself is liable, but for this sin, suffering may come even to his family and the entire world. Concerning other sins, if the sinner has other merits God will delay punishment up to three or four generations, but for this sin God metes out immediate punishment. Thus we see that even such things which are impervious to fire and water can be destroyed by the devastating power of a false oath.

Ravad (Hilchos Shavuos 11:13) notes that the Geonim instituted a new procedure in the Jewish courts: 'They forbade the taking of oaths with God's Name lest the entire world be brought to destruction by the sinners who swear falsely.'

◄§ **Fourth Commandment:**
To Remember the Sabbath

8. זָכוֹר אֶת־יוֹם הַשַּׁבָּת — *Remember the Sabbath day.*

Ramban explains the position of the Sabbath in the sequence of the Commandments:

First, God commanded that we believe in His existence, in His role as the Creator, Who knows, understands, and is the All-Powerful Controller of events. We are bidden to direct our faith to Him alone. Then God commanded that we adopt the Sabbath as a vivid sign and a perpetual acknowledgment that He alone created everything.

The description of the Sabbath as a 'remembrance' means that it should be the focal point of all our activities. The Talmud (*Beitzah* 16a) relates: They said of Shammai the Elder that all his life he ate in honor of the Sabbath. How so? If he purchased a beautiful animal, he would say, 'This will be in honor of the Sabbath.' If he found a more beautiful one the next day, he designated the second one for the Sabbath and used the first one for a weekday.

The *Mechilta* teaches that the Sabbath should be the highlight of a Jew's week. *R' Yitzchak* says: 'Do not count days as others count them, rather you should count every weekday in relation to the Sabbath. *Ramban* elaborates: Other nations consider the weekdays to be unrelated to each other. Thus, they gave each day a separate name after one of the heavenly forces [i.e., Sunday means 'sun's day,' Monday means 'moon's day' and so on]. Israel, however, counts all days in

for his money, the other denied the transaction. The first man then said: 'It was not you that I trusted, but the Holy Name that was on your head.'

Distraught, the victim fell into a deep sleep during which the prophet Elijah appeared to him and said, 'Go to the wife of the thief and tell her the password her husband uses: "On Passover we eat leaven and on Yom Kippur we eat pork." Then ask her for the money.' He did so and she gave it to him. When her husband found out what happened he beat her and, realizing that they had been found out, they went back to their heathen ways.

reference to the Sabbath: 'One day toward the Sabbath; two days towards the Sabbath.' Thus, we fulfill the Commandment *Remember the Sabbath,* every day of the week.

The candles are lit before the Sabbath so that their radiance will remind us to usher in this day with profound reverence.

When the Sabbath arrives, one should study its laws, customs and philosophical concepts, thereby heightening his awareness of its sanctity.

One should take care to avoid conversations that would distract him from the sanctity of the Sabbath. Discussions of business affairs drag man's thoughts from the sacred, spiritual realm of the Sabbath down to the profane, mundane weekday world.

Likewise, one should banish from his mind all worries and cares. In order to properly remember the joy of the Sabbath one must forget sad and mournful thoughts *(Sefer Chassidim).*

◄§ Remember/Observe

זָכוֹר — *Remember.*

In the repetition of the Ten Commandments *(Deuteronomy 5:12)* this verse reads שָׁמוֹר, *Observe the Sabbath Day.*

Ramban explains that *Remember* is a positive commandment to perform acts that enhance the sanctity of the Sabbath. *Observe* is a negative commandment which warns us to prevent and refrain from desecration of the Sabbath. With reference to these differing texts, the Rabbis *(Mechilta; Shavuos 20b)* taught: *Remember* and *Observe* were both spoken in a single utterance: Saying two words simultaneously is a miraculous superhuman feat which no mouth can accomplish and no

ear can hear. As the Sages explain, though God made only one utterance, Israel heard the two separate commandments. With this in mind, the Psalmist extols the Almighty *(Psalms 62:12), Once has God spoken; twice have I heard this — that strength belongs to God.* The purpose of this miracle was to demonstrate that the themes of honoring the Sabbath in a positive manner and avoiding its desecration are interconnected.

Ramban goes on to explain the status of women with regard to Sabbath observance. As a general rule, women are required to observe *all* negative commandments, but they are absolved from the observance of מִצְוַת עֲשֵׂה שֶׁהַזְּמַן גְּרָמָא, *a positive commandment dependent on a particular time.* Only if the Torah clearly obligates them to observe such commandments are they required to do so. Accordingly, women would be responsible not to *transgress* the Sabbath, but they would not be required to observe it in such positive ways as proclaiming its sanctity through the recitation of *Kiddush,* beautiful dress, or better food. Sabbath is one of the exceptions in which women *are* obligated in all its aspects, even though it is a positive commandment. We derive this from the fact that the positive and negative commandments were given in a single utterance; thus implying that both have the same status and are equally incumbent on everyone. Since women are obligated in this — as in *all* — negative commandments, they are required to *remember* the Sabbath, as well. Therefore, for example, women are as obligated as men to proclaim the sanctity of the Sabbath by reciting the *Kiddush (Shavuos 20b).*

The Talmud *(Shabbos 33b)* tells

of an old man who ran through the street before the beginning of the Sabbath holding two bunches of fragrant myrtle twigs. When bystanders asked him to explain this custom, he replied that he was running out to greet the Sabbath with this pleasant fragrance. The bystanders then asked, 'But why isn't one bundle sufficient?'

The old man replied, 'One bunch alludes to the command *Remember*, the other bunch alludes to the command *Observe.*'

When R' Shimon bar Yochai heard of this incident, he exclaimed to his son, 'Behold how precious every command is to the Jewish people!'[1]

לְקַדְּשׁוֹ — *To sanctify it.*

From this we learn that a special proclamation of קִידּוּשׁ, *sanctification*, should be pronounced at the outset of the Sabbath. This is the proper way to *remember* the Sabbath. Although the Torah's requirement is satisfied with a verbal proclamation like the one in the Sabbath prayers, the Rabbis enhanced the *mitzvah* by requiring that *Kiddush* be recited over a cup of wine, the beverage of divine joy *(Pesachim* 106a, 107a).

Rambam teaches that Sanctification of the Sabbath mean a clear demonstration of the supremacy of the seventh day over all the days that precede it and all the days that follow it. This is accomplished by reciting benedictions over this blessed and hallowed day both at the beginning of the Sabbath [*Kiddush*] and at its conclusion [*Havdalah*] to distinguish it from the weekdays on either side *(Sefer HaMitzvos* and *Hil. Shabbos* 29:1).

Mechilta observes: Display the uniqueness of the Sabbath! Dress differently, eat differently, drink differently!

If you wish to experience something of the spiritual existence of the World to Come, sanctify the Sabbath *(Osios D'R' Akiva).*

R' Shimon bar Yochai taught *(Bereishis Rabbah* 22:8): The first six days of the week consist of three sets of two days each. The Sabbath protested before God, 'Each day has a mate, but I have no mate!'

God replied, 'The Jewish nation is your mate.'

At Sinai, God commanded the Jewish people, 'Remember I told the Sabbath that you would be its mate.'

This Midrashic interpretation is based on the relationship between the word לְקַדְּשׁוֹ, *to sanctify it*, and קִדּוּשִׁין, *betrothal.* Thus, the Midrash derives from our verse that the Sabbath and Israel are, so to speak, 'betrothed' to one another *(Maharzu).*

The *Chofetz Chaim* taught that

---

1. The *Maggid of Dubno* notes that certain groups of people differentiate between these two major Sabbath themes. The pauper can easily observe the commandment not to desecrate the Sabbath, for he has no business enterprises that would suffer from closing down for a day. On the other hand, his poverty makes the positive commandment very difficult for him, for he cannot afford to buy wine, meat, fish, candles and clothes and all that is necessary to honor and remember the Sabbath properly.

On the other hand, the magnate easily and happily spends all that is necessary to increase Sabbath pleasure and enhance its splendor. The commandment to observe it, however, he fulfills grudgingly, because shutting down all his affairs on the Sabbath seems to cause financial losses.

Therefore, the Almighty emphasized the equality of both commands by proclaiming them simultaneously in one utterance. The rich man must *observe* the Sabbath with the same gusto and enthusiasm that he *remembers* it. Moreover, he must give generously to the poor to help them *remember* the Sabbath just as they *observe* it.

יָמִים֮ תַּעֲבֹד֒ וְעָשִׂ֖יתָ כָּל־מְלַאכְתֶּֽךָ׃
י וְי֙וֹם֙ הַשְּׁבִיעִ֔י שַׁבָּ֖ת ׀ לַיהוָ֣ה אֱלֹהֶ֑יךָ
לֹֽא־תַעֲשֶׂ֣ה כָל־מְלָאכָ֡ה אַתָּ֣ה ׀ וּבִנְךָֽ

the exhortation לְקַדְּשׁוֹ, to sanctify it represents a level of Sabbath involvement surpassing the preliminary stages of Remember and Observe. A Jew can perfunctorily discharge his duty to Remember and Observe the Sabbath by absent-mindedly performing a few familiar rituals and casually observing a few annoying restrictions — but such a Sabbath is sorely lacking in sanctity.

To hallow the Sabbath, one must make it the very essence of his being, the soul of his time. He must immerse himself in its powerful spirit and thrill to its sensation. The Jew should use every precious moment of the Sabbath to lift himself closer and closer to God.

9. שֵׁשֶׁת יָמִים תַּעֲבֹד — Six days you are to work.

Just as the Jewish people are obligated to rest on the seventh day, so are they obligated to work on the six days preceding it (Mechilta D'Rashbi).

And if a person has no work, let him find work! If he has an abandoned property, let him build on it; if he has a desolate field, let him revitalize it (Avos D'Rabbi Nosson 11.)

Sforno notes that the word תַּעֲבֹד is cognate to the word עֶבֶד, slave. Just as a slave works for a master and derives no personal benefit from his productivity, a person should recognize that his striving during the weekdays brings him no permanent profit; this world is only temporarily his. That is how a Jew

should view his weekday labor: he works out of necessity, but his spiritual labors on the Sabbath are truly his, for they remain eternally his (see also Ramban below).

[In the six weekdays the children of Israel are God's partners in Creation by working to improve and enhance everything that God fashioned. On the seventh day they rest together with the Almighty and proclaim that He is King.]

וְעָשִׂיתָ כָּל־מְלַאכְתֶּךָ — And accomplish all your tasks.

Keep busy all week but when the seventh day arrives all labor must come to a halt. Not only must the body cease its physical exertion, even the mind must rest from its mundane preoccupations. When the Sabbath begins, one must feel as if all his weekday tasks are completed and there is nothing left to think about — except the sanctity of the Sabbath (Rashi).

These words are a divine assurance to those who observe the Sabbath. Some people may complain that Judaism leaves over too little time for productive and profitable work. One day out of seven is 'wasted', and even in the remaining six days the spiritual demands on our time are heavy.

In reply God promises: 'Dedicate your lives to Me and to the consecration of My Sabbath day and I guarantee you that for no more than six days need you work in order to accomplish all your tasks.' However, the converse also holds true. Someone who lacks faith in this

days you are to work and accomplish all your tasks.
10 But the seventh day is Sabbath to HASHEM, your
God; you may not do any work — you, your son,

promise and encroaches upon the time allotted to God's service will fail in all his undertakings and find that he never has time enough for his business affairs *(R' Bachya; Alshich)*.

Ramban explains the difference between the two terms for work used in this verse — [תַּעֲבֹד] עֲבֹדָה and [מְלַאכְתֶּךָ] מְלָאכָה. עֲבֹדָה refers to labor that affords no immediate benefit to the laborer, such as work in fields or construction, while מְלָאכָה refers to such work as cooking, which gives immediate pleasure. Thus, our verse says that although man must do unpleasant work [עֲבֹדָה] as well as work that affords him benefit and pleasure [מְלָאכָה] during the week, on the Sabbath *(v. 10)* he must refrain from *all* forbidden work, even from that which provides for his immediate needs.

10. וְיוֹם הַשְּׁבִיעִי שַׁבָּת לַה' אֱלֹהֶיךָ — *But the seventh day is Sabbath* [lit. *cessation*] *to HASHEM, your God.*

Whoever ceases from labor on the seventh day offers testimony *to HASHEM,* verifying that He created the world in six days and rested on the seventh *(Midrash Lekach Tov).*

R' Yonah admonishes: Do not cease from work like an idle man who lounges with nothing to do. Your Sabbath rest must be dedica-

ted *to HASHEM, your God!* Utilize this free time for great spiritual activity. Engage in Torah study and marvel over the wonders of the Creator.

Pesikta Rabbasi rules: Let your cessation from labor on the Sabbath resemble God's cessation from labor. God created the world with the utterances of His mouth, and **He** refrained from such speech on the seventh day; so must you refrain from unnecessary speech on the seventh day. The Rabbis related that R' Shimon bar Yochai would remind his mother, 'Mother, it is the Sabbath,' and she would be silent.

R' Eivu taught that not only should one control his actions and words on the Sabbath but he should curb his thoughts as well.[1]

לֹא־תַעֲשֶׂה כָל־מְלָאכָה — *You may not do any work.*

Although מְלָאכָה is translated *work* for lack of a more accurate word, the translation gives only an approximation of the nature of the prohibition. As is obvious from some familiar laws of the Sabbath, it is quite common for great exertion to be permitted while seemingly negligible acts are forbidden. For example, the serving of many guests at a festive meal is surely a strenuous task, but it is permitted, while it is forbidden to go outdoors

1. This discipline is illustrated by the following incident: Once a pious man strolled through his vineyard on the Sabbath to inspect his property. He noticed a breach in a section of the wall and decided to repair it right after the Sabbath. Later he regretted this decision for he felt that he had profaned the day's sanctity by planning his weekday activities. Wishing to penalize himself for his infraction, he resolved never to mend this breach.

The Holy One, Blessed be He, rewarded him amply for his devotion. A huge fruit tree grew in that breach and filled in the gap, and the pious man profited generously from the income he derived from the tree's abundant fruit [see *Shabbos* 150a].

carrying a handkerchief or a key. Similarly, the same transgression is involved whether one flips a light switch or laboriously creates a fire by striking stones to make sparks. *R' Hirsch* notes that the word מְלָאכָה appears in Scripture nearly two hundred times, but *never* indicates strenuous work.

The definition of forbidden labors on the Sabbath is derived from the constructive labor that was required in the building of the מִשְׁכָּן, *Tabernacle*, in the Wilderness. The Sages isolated thirty-nine major categories of labor in the construction of the Tabernacle, and those are the categories prohibited on the Sabbath as well *(Shabbos* 49b).

R' Hirsch explains that the underlying nature of these prohibited acts is that they represent the intelligent carrying out of an intention. Thus, in order to violate the Torah's prohibition, the act must be intentional, constructive, done in the usual manner and so on. In this connection, it is instructive to note that the word מְלָאכָה is cognate with מַלְאָךְ, *angel*. An angel is a being that exists solely to serve a purpose — the fulfillment of God's will. So, too, the labors of the Sabbath involve the carrying out of an intention, rather than becoming fatigued.

[The definitions and laws of the individual labors are voluminous and beyond the scope of this commentary, but it is essential to note that they are not related to exertion.]

When the Jewish people forsook God and worshiped idols in Egypt, they implied a belief that His Presence was not supreme everywhere on earth, but that various deities were supreme in their own locations. Therefore, God bade Israel to build a Tabernacle that would symbolize the world in microcosm. The Presence of the Almighty filled the Tabernacle unmistakably and He declared, 'Just as My Presence permeates every inch of the Tabernacle, the miniature world, so too, it pervades every area and atom of the entire world though it is hidden from human perception.' Seen in this light, the Tabernacle symbolizes all of creation, and the forms of constructive work that went into its building are symbolic of God's own creation of the universe. Therefore, a fitting testimony to our acknowledgment of God as the Creator Who refrained from work on the Sabbath is that we withdraw from the type of work with which the Tabernacle was built. *(R' Yitzchok Hutner, Kuntres HaShabbos*, essay 6)

אַתָּה וּבִנְךָ וּבִתֶּךָ — *You, (and) your son, (and) your daughter.*

This command obligates parents to supervise their children who are still minors and under parental jurisdiction. It cannot refer to children who have already reached the age of *bar mitzvah*, since they are personally responsible to observe this commandment like all others *(Mechilta).* [1]

1. A Jew once came to the *Chofetz Chaim* for a blessing. Unfortunately, this man's son did not observe the Sabbath. The *tzaddik* responded to his request, saying, 'Who am I to give blessings? I am only a simple Jew. If you really want blessings you have to go to the holy Sabbath, for this most sacred of days is a source of blessing. But it is not enough to observe the Sabbath yourself, it must be a family affair. The wording of the Sabbath commandment is unique, for here Scripture emphasizes: *You, your son, your daughter.* Nowhere else does the

your daughter, your manservant, your maidservant, your animal, and the convert within your gates —

The Talmud (Yevamos 114a) rules that a parent may not tell his child to carry anything for him through the public domain.

A parent may not instruct his child, 'Bring me this vessel from the market place, bring me that fruit basket from the market place.' If a child comes to extinguish a light a parent should not permit him to do so (Mechilta D'Rashbi).

In the light of the above, Sefer Chassidim explains the juxtaposition in one verse of the mitzvos to revere parents and observe the Sabbath (Leviticus 19:3). What is the prime cause of strict Sabbath observance? Respect for father and mother! When a young child attempts to desecrate the Sabbath his parents should stop him. Conversely, if parents firmly enforce Sabbath observance in their homes, their reward will be that their children will truly respect them.

עַבְדְּךָ וַאֲמָתְךָ — Your manservant, your maidservant.

Mechilta observes that this does not refer to Jewish slaves because they remain full-fledged Jews despite their servitude and are obligated to fulfill all commandments. Thus there is no reason to specify that a master should not

work his Jewish slaves on the Sabbath. Rather our verse refers to gentiles who were sold to Jews and entered into the בְּרִית, covenant, males by means of circumcision and immersion, and females by means of immersion alone. Such slaves are obligated to observe all the Torah laws that are incumbent upon women. As indicated by our verse, their master has a personal obligation to insure that they rest on the Sabbath.

וּבְהֶמְתֶּךָ — Your animal.

[The word בְּהֵמָה can refer either to all animals or only domesticated animals, depending on the context. Therefore, when it appears together with the word חַיָּה, which usually refers to non-domesticated animals, בְּהֵמָה is interpreted to mean such animals as cattle and sheep. In our verse, we translate your animal, because the prohibition against working an animal on the Sabbath is not limited to farm animals.]

A person may not permit his animal to work or carry a load on the Sabbath, nor may he lend or rent his animals to a non-Jew who will work them on the Sabbath. [These laws are set forth at length in Orach Chaim 246.][2]

Torah warn a person about his family. It does not say: You shall not eat pork, you, your son, your daughter. Nor does it say: You shall wear tzitzis, you, your son, your daughter. Certainly every parent is responsible for his children's observance of the entire Torah, but for the Sabbath this duty is greater than for everything else' (HaDeah V'HaDibbur, vol. III, p. 287).

2. Pesikta Rabbasi (Parshas Parah 2) tells of a Jew who sold his ox to a non-Jew. After working all week, the ox refused to work on the Sabbath day when it was accustomed to rest in the house of its former Jewish master. Upset by this behavior, the gentile wanted to cancel the sale. The Jew came and whispered in the ear of the ox, 'When you were in my possession, I was prohibited to work you on the Sabbath, but now that you belong to the gentile you must work even on the Seventh.' The ox obeyed. The gentile was so impressed by this incident that he converted and eventually became a Torah scholar known as R' Yochanan ben Torasa, which means (in Aramaic) son of the ox, in appreciation of the fact that the behavior of an ox had inspired his spiritual rebirth.

יא אֲשֶׁר בִּשְׁעָרֶיךָ: כִּי שֵׁשֶׁת־יָמִים עָשָׂה
יהוה אֶת־הַשָּׁמַיִם וְאֶת־הָאָרֶץ אֶת־הַיָּם
וְאֶת־כָּל־אֲשֶׁר־בָּם וַיָּנַח בַּיּוֹם הַשְּׁבִיעִי
עַל־כֵּן בֵּרַךְ יהוה אֶת־יוֹם הַשַּׁבָּת

The second version of the commandments (Deuteronomy 5:14) includes an addition: Your ox and your ass and your every animal [see Bava Kama 54b].

Meshech Chochmah explains that the first version cites the reason for Sabbath rest as a remembrance of God's 'rest' after the six days of Creation. Since all types of animals were created in that period it is obvious that all your cattle, no matter of what species, should rest. The second version, however, offers the Exodus from Egypt as the reason for Sabbath rest. When people see even the animals resting on Sabbath they will remember that God allowed us to rest from the Egyptian slavery. However, one might think that the ox and the ass need not 'testify' to the redemption by means of Sabbath rest, because they are used in a different mitzvah that commemorates the Exodus. The Torah ruled that a firstborn ox is sacrificed and a firstborn ass must be redeemed [Exodus 34:19, 20]. Therefore, the Torah must specify these two in particular, to stress that despite their firstborn sanctity, they are included in the directive of Sabbath rest.

וְגֵרְךָ אֲשֶׁר בִּשְׁעָרֶיךָ — And the convert within your gates.

Mechilta identifies this person as a גֵּר צֶדֶק, righteous convert, who becomes a Jew and accepts all the mitzvos of the Torah. [Sometimes the Torah uses the word גֵּר to refer

to a גֵּר תּוֹשָׁב, resident non-Jew, who is permitted to live in Eretz Yisrael on the basis of his pledge to observe the seven Noachide laws. Such a gentile is not required to observe the Sabbath. The righteous convert is described as within your gates because a halachically legal conversion must be performed in the presence of a בֵּית דִּין, (beis din), court, composed of three members. The term your gates is often used to refer to the court because it was customary for the beis din to convene at the city gates (see Deuteronomy 16:18). This verse also implies that the convert is welcomed and accepted into the community gates and participates fully in the Sanctification of the Sabbath despite his gentile, unsacred origin.]

11. כִּי שֵׁשֶׁת־יָמִים עָשָׂה ה' — For [in] six days HASHEM made.

The clause does not include the prepositional prefix ב,in — [בְּ]שֵׁשֶׁת, [in] six. Rather it says, שֵׁשֶׁת יָמִים, literally, six days HASHEM made, implying that God created the very days. The reason for this unusual construction is to indicate that even the concept of time — the existence of days, hours, and minutes — had to be created by God. Before God created the universe, there was only a timeless unstructured eternity. When God brought heaven and earth into existence, He also created the dimension of time. Our verse indicates that God ordained the Sabbath to be the 'soul' of time and the

11 *for in six days HASHEM made the heavens, the earth, the sea and all that is in them, and He rested on the seventh day. Therefore, HASHEM blessed the Sabbath day and sanctified it.*

focal point of the Jewish calendar (R' Bachya).

Here the Torah describes the Sabbath as a remembrance of Creation. In the second version *(Deuteronomy 5:15)*, the Torah gives a different reason, saying: *And remember that you were a servant in the land of Egypt and that HASHEM, your God, brought you out of there with a mighty arm and an outstretched hand. Therefore, HASHEM your God, commanded you to make the Sabbath day* [see *Moreh Nevuchim*, II:32].

Meshech Chochmah (Va'eschanan) explains that the main purpose of the Sabbath rest is to commemorate God's role as Creator of the universe [as stated in the first version]. If so, even the gentile nations should be obligated to observe the Sabbath, for they, too, must recognize God as the Creator.

The second version of the Commandments, therefore, explains the unique relationship of Israel to the Sabbath. Other nations did not witness a vivid revelation of God's role as Supreme Controller of Creation, but Israel did. Through the ten plagues He inflicted upon Egypt, God demonstrated His mastery over every area of nature to Israel. Since Jewish nationhood was born at that time, when God manifested Himself in His continuing role of Creator, it is the singular mission of Israel to observe the Sabbath as a means of promulgating this truth [see *Ramban, Deuteronomy 5:15*].

אֶת־הַשָּׁמַיִם וְאֶת־הָאָרֶץ אֶת־הַיָּם וְאֶת־כָּל־אֲשֶׁר־בָּם — *The heavens, the earth, the sea and all that is in them.*

Mechilta D'Rashbi notes that the sea is part of the globe, and need not be mentioned separately. The Torah mentions it only to emphasize that the sea's importance is equal to that of both heaven and earth combined. *Meshech Chochmah* explains that the sea is always equated with purity and enjoys the intensive presence of God because, on the whole, it remains untainted and undefiled by human exploitation.

וַיָּנַח בַּיּוֹם הַשְּׁבִיעִי — *And He rested on the seventh day.*

Mechilta wonders: Does God Almighty really need rest? The prophet says of God, *The eternal God HASHEM — the Creator of the ends of the earth — fatigues not, nor is He weary ... He infuses the weary ones with strength and increases the energy of the exhausted (Isaiah 40:28-29).*

Rather, Scripture refers to God in human terms to emphasize the significance of the Sabbath. If God, Who needs no rest, rested on the seventh day, certainly man *who is born to toil (Job 5:7)* should cease his labor on this holy day.

עַל־כֵּן בֵּרַךְ ה' אֶת־יוֹם הַשַּׁבָּת וַיְקַדְּשֵׁהוּ — *Therefore, HASHEM blessed the Sabbath day and sanctified it.*

God blessed and sanctified the Sabbath by endowing people with an increased spiritual capacity that enables Jews to accept a higher

כַּבֵּד   יב וַיְקַדְּשֵׁהוּ:
אֶת־אָבִיךָ וְאֶת־אִמֶּךָ לְמַעַן יַאֲרִכוּן

degree of wisdom and insight than they can at other times *(Ibn Ezra)*.

According to *Rav Saadiah Gaon* the blessing and sanctification prophetically refer to those who observe the sanctity of the Sabbath, for they will be blessed and sanctified.

Ramban, however, explains that the blessing of the Sabbath is the fountain of all blessing, and is the foundation of the world; God sanctified it by having it draw from the Sanctity above.

According to *Radak*, 'blessing' is abundant well-being brought about by the Sabbath. It is the day when, free from mundane worry, man can immerse himself in wisdom and spirituality. God thus blessed this day by commanding the Jews themselves to rest on it and hallow it. He sanctified it by distinguishing it from ordinary days. It is the day during which the Jews abstain from work as a sign between them and God that they are holy by virtue of their observance of the Sabbath which testifies to the divine creation of the world.

Rashi perceives this verse as having been written in anticipation of the future: He blessed it through the manna, a double portion of which fell on the sixth day in preparation of the Sabbath; and sanctified it through the manna, none of which fell on the Sabbath [see *Exodus* 16:22.] (Cf. *Mechilta*).

Or HaChaim agrees that the *Midrash* quoted by *Rashi* is an allusion to future events, but the plain meaning of the verse is that God gave the Sabbath a blessing that

raised it above vicissitudes of this world. Creation demands labor to provide food, drink, and all the other human necessities. Such labor is forbidden on the Sabbath while simultaneously the Sabbath is honored through three prescribed meals and more physical indulgence than weekdays. God blessed the Sabbath with abundance despite the abstinence from 'necessary' labor. What is more, the sanctity of the Sabbath provides the blessing of success for the activity of the weekdays.

Mechilta cites the opinion of R' Shimon who says: God sanctified the Sabbath בִּמְאוֹר פָּנִים שֶׁל אָדָם, *through the luminous face of man.* God endows the face of the Sabbath observer with a spiritual luminescence, demonstrating that God's holy spirit rests upon him.

[The blessing of Sabbath, it must be noted, was that it was endowed with a spiritual exaltation, a sanctity which distinguishes it from all other days. In contrast to the festivals which were dependent upon the observance by witnesses of the new moon and of the calendary calculations of the rabbinical courts, the Sabbath was imbued with its *own* sanctity — independent of human activity. This holiness was endowed by the Creator, Who ordained that it continually and faithfully manifest itself every seventh day without interruption in testimony to God's sovereignty over the universe.]

The 'blessing' was that people would not experience need because of not working on Shabbos: *It is the*

עשרת הדברות [48]

blessing of HASHEM *that makes rich* (Proverbs 10:22; *Minchah Belulah*).

◆§ Fifth Commandment: To honor parents

בַּבֵּד אֶת־אָבִיךָ וְאֶת־אִמֶּךָ — *Honor your father and mother.*[1]

Ramban explains: With the Fourth Commandment God completed the description of man's obligations directly to honor the Creator. Now God commands us concerning our obligations towards His creatures, beginning with duties to our parents, who resemble the Creator in a sense, because they are God's partners in the creation of a child. It is as if God is our primary parent and father and mother complete the task of bringing us into life. For this reason, the repetition of the Commandments (*Deuteronomy 5:16*) adds a phrase: *Honor your father and your mother ...* בַּאֲשֶׁר צִוְּךָ ה׳ אֱלֹהֶיךָ, *as HASHEM, your God, commanded you;* 'Just as I have issued commands concerning My honor, so do I now command you concerning the honor of those who joined Me in your creation.'

Ramban continues: the Torah does not define the 'honor' due to parents, because we are to derive it from the preceding verses that describe the honor due to the ultimate Parent, God. A person must acknowledge his true parents as his creators and not identify others as his parents. One should not honor his parents for ulterior motives, such as a wish to inherit their estate

or to derive some other personal gain. Nor should someone swear vainly or falsely by the life of his father or mother. As the Sages teach, giving honor to one's parents is likened to giving honor to God Himself (*Kiddushin 30b*).

[*Ramban's* thesis explains why this commandment was inscribed on the first tablet with the commandments concerned with the honor of God. The Talmud (*Kiddushin 31b*) relates that when Rav Yosef heard his mother's footsteps he would say, 'Let me arise before the approach of the שְׁכִינָה, *Divine Presence.*']

The Rabbis taught: There are three partners in the creation of a human being, the Almighty, his father and his mother (*Kiddushin 30b*). When someone honors his father and mother, the Lord says, 'I reckon it as though I dwelled with them and they honored Me.' When someone pains his parents, the Lord says, 'I have done wisely not to dwell with them, for had I done so, they would pain Me as well' (*Kiddushin 31a*).

Haamek Davar explains that the added phrase in the second version, *as HASHEM, your God, commanded you,* is meant to place the *mitzvah* in a clearer perspective. Someone may tend to honor his parents merely because of sentimentality or a sense of moral obligation toward them. The Torah stresses, however, that one must fulfill this *mitzvah* regardless of personal feeling or

---

1. *In Psalms (138:4) we read: All the kings of the earth give thanks to You HASHEM because they heard the utterances of Your mouth.* Noting that the Psalmist did not use the singular form מַאֲמַר *utterance,* but the plural form אִמְרֵי, *utterances,* the Talmud (*Kiddushin 31a*) interprets this as a reference to the precepts of the Ten Commandments.

The Midrash (*Bamidbar Rabbah 8:4*) elaborates: When the kings of the world heard the

sensitivity. This command is no different from any other — it is mandatory because so has *HASHEM your God commanded you.*

The aforementioned sources emphasize that recognition of parents fosters recognition of the Creator. Other sources stress that gratitude to parents breeds gratitude for the kindness which God bestows upon man.

Sefer HaChinuch (Mitzvah 33) writes: At the root of this *mitzvah* lies the thought that it is proper for a man to acknowledge and bestow kindness upon someone who has done him good and that he should not be an ingrate who denies the good done him by another — for that is an evil trait, despicable to both God and man. A person should realize that his parents are the cause of his being in this world and therefore it is truly proper for him to give them every honor and benefit he can. For they gave birth to him and exerted themselves greatly on his behalf during his early years.

When someone successfully integrates into his personality the quality of expressing gratitude, it will be a stepping stone toward a higher appreciation of the goodness of God, the Prime Cause of his existence and of the entire human race. A person with a sense of gratitude will recognize that God formed his body and gave him a soul and intelligence. Otherwise, man would be *like a horse, like a mule, uncomprehending (Psalms 32:9).* When he realizes all this he will take special pains to serve and worship God to the utmost of his ability.

◄§ Honor and Reverence

The Torah expresses the obligations of the child to his parents in two separate commands: כַּבֵּד אֶת־אָבִיךָ וְאֶת־אִמֶּךָ, *Honor your father and mother,* and אִישׁ אִמּוֹ וְאָבִיו תִּירָאוּ, *Every man shall revere* [lit. *fear*] *his mother and his father (Leviticus 19:3).*

The Rabbis taught: What is *reverence* and what is *honor? Reverence* means that a child must neither stand nor sit in his parent's place, not contradict his words nor render a decision against him. *Honor* means that he must serve his parent food and drink, clothe and cover him, and lead him in and out (*Kid-*

First Commandment, *I am HASHEM, your God,* they exclaimed, 'God is no different than us — no king wants anyone to deny his sovereignty!' When the kings heard the Second Commandment, *You shall not recognize others' gods,* they mocked it, saying, 'This God is like us; He tolerates no challenger to His authority.' When they heard the Third Commandment, *You shall not take the Name of HASHEM, your God, in vain,* they protested, 'There is nothing extraordinary about this; no king wants his subjects to swear falsely or vainly in his name.' They heard the Fourth Commandment, *Remember the Sabbath day to sanctify it.* This, too, they failed to appreciate saying, 'Every monarch wants his subjects to observe his holidays.'

But when the kings of the world heard the Fifth Commandment, *Honor your father and mother,* they were amazed. They exclaimed, 'This contradicts all our traditions, because we demand that our subjects display undivided loyalty to their liege lord by signing a solemn oath stating, "I hereby recognize no parent or relative; I pledge my allegiance exclusively to my king and master." '

Then, the kings came to recognize that God's commands are unselfish, unlike their own decrees, and they appreciated the wisdom and fairness of all the preceding commandments as well. Humbly, they arose from their thrones and offered homage and thanks to God.

The Talmud (*Kiddushin* 31a) concludes: This is the meaning of the verse (*Psalms 119:160*): רֹאשׁ־דְּבָרְךָ אֱמֶת, *the beginning of Your word is truth.* Is only the beginning true and not the end? Rather this was uttered by the kings who waited until they heard the commandments to their conclusion, and only after appreciating the later ones would they admit that even the first four commandments, 'the beginning of Your word,' are true and just.

dushin 31b). [In general terms, therefore, *reverence* forbids activities that would tend to reduce the esteem in which parents are held, while *honor* requires positive deeds for the convenience of parents and to raise their status.]

In the command to *honor*, the Torah places the father before the mother. In the command to *revere*, the Torah places the mother before the father. Why the differentiation?

God knows that the average person will give more honor to his mother than to his father. She pampers her children and speaks gently to them. The father, on the other hand, admonishes and punishes his children. Therefore, when the Torah speaks of honoring parents and giving them pleasure, it emphasizes the father first — lest a child be reluctant to honor the father who treated him harshly. But with respect to reverence — fear and respect — the opposite is true. It is natural for a child to fear his father more than his mother, therefore the Torah gives precedence to the mother in the *mitzvah* concerning

fear, to teach us that we must revere our mothers as much as our fathers (*Kiddushin* 31a; *Kerisos* 28a).

[The word כָּבוֹד, *honor*, is cognate with כָּבֵד, *heavy*. This implies that true honor involves taking parents very seriously and giving them the concern and attention worthy of a weighty' matter. To provide for a parent's needs is an expression of his value and worth.]

R' Shimon bar Yochai said: The most difficult of all *mitzvos* is, *Honor your father and mother* (*Tanchuma, Ekev* 2).

R' Yochanan said: Fortunate is he who never sets eyes on his parents [because it is virtually impossible to honor them adequately and one is punished for failure to do so (*Rashi*)]. When Rabbi Yochanan was conceived, his father died; when he was born, his mother died (*Kiddushin* 31b).[1]

Rambam (*Hilchos Mamrim* 6:7) sums up the scope of this command:

How far must one go to honor his father and mother? Even if they took a wallet full of gold pieces

---

1. The following incidents illustrate to what lengths the rabbis of the Talmud would go to honor their parents:

R' Tarfon's mother was walking in the courtyard one Sabbath day when her shoe tore and came off. Rabbi Tarfon hurried and placed his hands under her feet, as she walked, until she reached her couch.

Once, when he fell ill and the rabbis came to visit him, his mother said to them, 'Pray for my son, R' Tarfon, for he serves me with excessive honor,' and told them of the above incident.

They responded, 'Even if your son were to do a thousand times more he would not yet have bestowed even half the honor demanded by the Torah' (*Yerushalmi Peah* 1:1).

Rabban Shimon ben Gamliel said, 'I served my father all my life, but I did not extend to him even one-hundredth of the honor given to Isaac by his son Esau. For I would serve my father even in soiled clothing and when I went out to attend to my affairs I would change to clean clothes, but Esau always dressed royally and immaculately to serve his father' (*Bereishis Rabbah* 65:16).

R' Abahu said: 'My son Abimi perfectly fulfilled the commandment of filial respect.'

Abimi had five sons who were all ordained during R' Abahu's lifetime. Nevertheless, whenever R' Abahu would arrive at Abimi's door, Abimi would run personally to open the door, saying 'Yes, I am coming! Yes, I am coming!' until he reached it. Once R' Abahu asked for a drink of water. By the time Abimi brought it, the older man dozed off. Abimi remained bent over his father [drink in hand] until he awakened (*Kiddushin* 31b).

They asked Rabbi Eliezer: 'How far must one go with honoring parents?'

He replied: 'Go and learn from the conduct of a gentile from Ashkelon, named Dama ben Nesinah, who had a precious stone that was needed for the vestments of the *Kohen Gadol*

יָמֶיךָ עַל הָאֲדָמָה אֲשֶׁר־יהוה אֱלֹהֶיךָ
נֹתֵן לָךְ: יג לֹא תִּרְצָח לֹא

from him and threw it into the sea before his very eyes, he must not shame them, show pain before them, nor display anger to them. Rather he must accept the decree of Scripture and keep silent.

And how far must one go in his fear and reverence? Even if he is dressed in precious clothes and is sitting in a place of honor before many people, and his parents come and tear his clothes, hit him on the head and spit in his face, he may not shame them, but must remain silent, and be in awe and fear of the King of Kings who commanded him to do so. For if a flesh and blood king had decreed that he do something even more painful than this, he could not hesitate to obey. How much more so, then, when he is commanded by Him Who created the world at His will!

לְמַעַן יַאֲרִכוּן יָמֶיךָ עַל הָאֲדָמָה אֲשֶׁר־ 'אֱלֹהֶיךָ נֹתֵן לָךְ — So that you may live a long life [lit. so that your days be lengthened] upon the land which HASHEM, your God, gives you.

R' Bachya cites R' Saadiah Gaon who comments: The reward for filial piety is long life ... because it may happen that parents will live for a long time and become a heavy burden upon their children, who may grow weary of this 'honor'. The reward for this mitzvah, therefore, is so that you will live

long. Consequently, children should realize that if they regret the longevity of their parents [thereby losing the reward for the mitzvah], they will actually be regretting their own future longevity.

Pa'aneach Razah notes that the letter ן, nun, at the end of יַאֲרִכוּן is superfluous. He comments that the suffix nun can mean they. Thus our verse would be rendered that in the merit of the honor you show your parents they [your parents] will lengthen your days, because they will gratefully pray for your welfare.

Rambam suggests that acknowledgment of parental authority reinforces the fabric of human society as a whole and enhances the quality of life for all of society's members. One who makes an enduring contribution to the welfare of this world deserves the opportunity to enjoy life for a long time. He comments (Peah 1:1) that this mitzvah falls into the category of those which are designed to aid in the establishment of stable social relationships. One who performs such mitzvos is rewarded in the future world for fulfilling a mitzvah, but in addition he benefits in this world for having benefited his fellow men. If he pursues such a path and his neighbor behaves similarly, all will share the common good in this world.

[High Priest]. The rabbis came to Dama and offered him a fortune for it, but the key to the jewel-box was under his sleeping father's head and Dama refused to disturb him. The rabbis left and bought a gem elsewhere. The following year God rewarded Dama and a rare Parah Adumah [Red Cow] needed in the Temple service, was born in his herd. When the rabbis came to him to purchase it, he said, "I know that I can demand of you all the money in the world and you will pay it — but I ask only for the amount I forfeited by honoring my father'' ' (Kiddushin 31a).

live a long life upon the land which HASHEM, *your God, gives you.*
13 *You shall not kill.*

[Longevity is an appropriate reward for filial devotion because the respectful child accepts the traditions handed down by his parents and insures their perpetuation. The longer such a faithful child lives, the better the chance that the tradition he represents will be transferred to the next generation.]

Ralbag writes: Respect for parents will ensure that succeeding generations will accept the teachings of their elders, generation after generation, with the result that they will all be strong in their observance of God's Torah. Also this will help perfect the home, which is the first step towards perfecting of the state. This also insures Israel's continued loyalty to Torah.

In the second version of the commandments *(Deuteronomy 5:16)* an additional phrase is inserted into the stated reward for the devoted child — *so that you may live a long life* וּלְמַעַן יִיטַב לָךְ, *and so that it may be good for you.* The Talmud *(Bava Kamma 54b)* explains why this assurance is lacking in the first version: God knew that the first tablets were destined to be shattered by Moses. Had the promise of good life been included in the first version, it would have appeared as if Israel's hopes for a good life were

shattered with the tablets. God, therefore, saved this special promise for the second tablets, which were a lasting testament.

Baal HaTurim (Deuteronomy 5:16) notes that the second version of the Ten Commandments is slightly longer than the first and contains seventeen extra letters. The number seventeen is the numerical equivalent of the word טוב, *goodness,* which is the reward introduced in the second version.

Elsewhere, the Talmud *(Kiddushin 39b; Chullin 142a)* interprets these assurances as being reserved for the future world of eternal reward, explaining: *So that your days be lengthened* in the world of endless length; *and so that it might be good for you* in the world which is entirely good, without any admixture of sorrow or evil.

◆§ Sixth Commandment: Prohibition against murder[1]

13. לֹא תִרְצָח — *You shall not kill.*

God said to Israel, 'My nation, do not be murderers. Do not consort nor enter into partnership with murderers, lest your children learn the ways of those who shed blood. It is because of the sin of bloodshed that the sword of war comes to the world' *(Targum Yonasan).*

1. In response to a question by the Roman Emperor Hadrian, R' Yehoshua ben Chananyah explained why God's Name is not mentioned in connection with any of the last five commandments. He likened the matter to Hadrian's own policy of placing his statue, likeness, or coat-of-arms on virtually every building in the kingdom — but he would not permit his name to be associated with an outhouse or other degraded place. Similarly, God associated His Name with the commandments of the first Tablet, which spoke of belief and honor to him and parents. But He would not associate His holy Name directly with such heinous sins as murder, adultery, kidnapping, false testimony, and greedy desire *(Pesikta Rabbasi 21).*

A soul which you cannot bring back to life — why should you destroy it? A candle which you are powerless to rekindle — why should you extinguish it? O murderer! You can conceal yourself from the eyes of flesh and blood, but you cannot hide from the all-pervading vision of God! The innocent victim of bloodshed is destined to stand before the heavenly tribunal to point an accusing finger at his assailant. The slain man will condemn the murderer before God Who will sentence the killer to the fires of Gehinnom (*Midrash Asseres Ha-Dibros*).

Mechilta explains that when God gave the Ten Commandments He etched them on two matching tablets of stone — five commandments on each. The second set of five corresponds to the first set. The Sixth Commandment, *You shall not kill* is parallel to the First Commandment, *I am HASHEM your God*. This juxtaposition teaches that whoever sheds blood is regarded as if he had impaired the Divine likeness [for man was created in the image of God]. This may be compared to a king of flesh and blood who conquered a country and sought to establish his authority. He put up pictures of himself, erected statues in his likeness, and minted coins engraved with his image. A while later the people rebelled against the king. Because they could not strike at his person, they tore down his pictures, smashed his statues and defaced his coins. Similarly, the murderer defies God by attacking the man who represents God's image. This idea is clearly expressed in the verse, *Whoever sheds the blood of man, by man shall his blood be shed; for in the image of God He* [God] *made man* (Genesis 9:6).

Seder Eliyahu Rabbah explains the juxtaposition of *You shall not kill* with *Honor your father and mother:* This alludes to a wealthy person who refuses to support his father and mother in their old age. God Almighty considers him to be tantamount to a murderer who slays his own parents time after time.[1]

R' Avrohom Yitzchak Bloch of Telshe offers a penetrating analysis into the unique nature of the Ten Commandments: Why was the prohibition against murder included in the Ten Commandments which were given only to Israel — is not murder a universal crime for which even non-Jews are liable? Indeed, murder is one of the seven Noachide laws!

In answer to this we must understand that the Jewish concept of murder is far more subtle and comprehensive than the universal defi-

---

1. *Midrash Asseres HaDibros* observes that after commanding children to honor their parents, the Torah cautions against over-zealousness in guarding the honor of parents: Perhaps a devoted child will say, 'Since I must honor my parents it is my duty to kill anyone who disgraces them!' Therefore, the Torah warns, *You shall not kill.* Or, perhaps the zealous child will say, 'This villain shamed my parents, therefore I will embarrass him by seducing his wife.' Therefore, the Torah commanded, *You shall not commit adultery.* A devoted child may say, 'This man disgraced my parents, I must avenge them by damaging his property.' Therefore the Torah commanded, *You shall not steal.* Finally, the angry child may say, 'I will avenge my parents by testifying falsely against the one who harmed them.' Therefore, the Torah warns *You shall not bear false witness against your neighbor.*

You shall not commit adultery.
You shall not steal.

nition. The Noachide prohibition is limited to the taking of life, but the Torah's prohibition alludes to many other things as well:

☐ The Talmud (*Bava Metzia* 58b) goes so far as to say that whoever publicly embarrasses his fellow man is considered as if he had shed blood because shame causes a person's blood to drain from his face.

☐ The man who forcibly assaults a betrothed or married woman is regarded as a murderer, as Scripture says, *for like one who rises up against his neighbor and kills him is this matter* [rape] *regarded (Deuteronomy 22:26).*

☐ A host is responsible for a traveler who leaves his home, and must provide him with sufficient provisions and a proper escort lest the traveler fall prey to hunger or attack. The host who fails to meet his obligations is described in the Torah as a shedder of blood (*Deuteronomy 21:17; Sotah* 45b-46b).

☐ One Jew who causes another to lose his livelihood is considered as having murdered him (*Yevamos* 78b).

☐ The Talmud (*Sotah* 22b) expounds upon a verse in *Proverbs* 7:26 which introduces yet another dimension in the Jewish concept of murder: כִּי־רַבִּים חֲלָלִים הִפִּילָה, *for she has cast down many corpses —* this refers to the immature student who has not attained the proper level of wisdom, yet dares to issue halachic decisions; וַעֲצֻמִים כָּל־ הֲרֻגֶיהָ, *and the number of her slain victims is enormous —* this refers to

the mature scholar who is qualified to make decisions and teach Torah, but refrains from doing so. Both of them commit crimes against the people and "kill', one actively, the other passively.

All of these crimes and many more are included under the concept of *You shall not kill*, although of course, they do not incur the death penalty.

⋅§ Seventh Commandment:
Prohibition against adultery

לֹא תִּנְאָף — *You shall not commit adultery.*

God said to Israel, 'My nation, do not be immoral. Do not consort nor enter into any form of partnership with immoral people and do not permit your children to enter their company lest they learn from their wicked deeds. As a punishment for immorality a plague ravishes the world, destroying righteous and wicked alike' (*Targum Yonasan*).

The very word תִּנְאָף, which is used to describe adultery, alludes to the enormity of the sin and its consequences because תִּנְאָף is a contraction of תֵּן אַף, *make anger;* the adulterer arouses the anger of God to a level of great intensity.

Ordinarily God is patient and long-suffering, but He does not restrain His anger against adulterers, as the prophet says: *And I* [God] *will be swift to testify against the sorcerers and the adulterers (Malachi 3:5).*

Adultery arouses God's anger more than other sins because the adulterer destroys the sacred harmony and tranquility of a contented marriage. The adulterer incites אַף, *anger*, and animosity between man and wife and this arouses the anger of God (*Bamidbar Rabbah* 10:2).

R' Shimon ben Tarfon said: A person should never be an agent or an intermediary for sin. Even if he merely arranges an immoral rendezvous he is considered an adulterer (*Shavuos* 47b).

Harav Mordechai Gifter develops the theme expounded by *R' Bloch* (see above with regard to the broader definition of murder.) Here, too, we find that the scope of the Jewish prohibition against adultery extends far beyond marital infidelity:

The Talmud (*Sanhedrin* 81a), based on a verse in *Ezekiel* 18:6, teaches that interference with a neighbor's livelihood is tantamount to defiling his wife. In making such a comparison, the Sages teach that the Torah's moral imperatives cannot be satisfied merely by avoidance of sin in its crassest form. The Torah demands that a Jew refrain from any acts — even relatively minor ones — that are outgrowths of the character flaws that are the root of major transgressions. As we have seen above, to inflict shame is related to murder; both result from disregard of another human being's personal dignity. In the case of adultery, while interfering with another's livelihood is a far cry from defiling his wife, both grow out of a disregard for the legitimate rights of another human being.

The best way to avoid tampering with what a neighbor holds most precious and intimate is to hold his every possession sacrosanct. A person who cannot bring himself to damage his neighbor in even a casual, indirect way will have insured himself against temptation to do him more direct harm [Artscroll *Ezekiel* 18:6, footnote].

The Seventh Commandment — the second to appear on the second tablet — corresponds to the Second Commandment on the first tablet: *You shall not recognize the gods of others before My presence*, because someone who betrays his spouse will eventually betray God Himself (*Mechilta*).

[Moreover, the prophets who admonished Israel for their sin of idol worship often compared the unfaithful nations to a harlot and an adulterous wife. The prophet lashes on: *Adulterous wife, Who under her husband takes strangers! ... Therefore, O harlot! Hear the word of HASHEM ... I will punish you with the punishment of an adultress* (*Ezekiel* 16:32,36,38).

⦿§ Eighth Commandment: Prohibition against stealing

לֹא תִגְנֹב — *You shall not steal.*

Midrash Asseres HaDibros issues a stern warning: Do not associate with thieves and stay far away from them, lest your children learn from their ways. Because of thievery, famine comes to the world. Let no stolen property cling to your hand because dishonesty will eventually bring mourning to every limb of your body. Moreover, the thief will come to despise himself, as it says (*Proverbs* 29:24) *He who shares with a thief despises his own life.* Because of theft beautiful homes are uprooted as the prophet says: *It* [the curse] *will descend upon the home of the thief ... and it shall remain inside the house and it shall consume its timber and its stones* (*Zechariah* 5:4).

Rashi comments: Here Scripture prohibits kidnapping, the 'stealing' of human beings. Later, in *Leviticus* 19:11, the Torah commands לֹא תִגְנֹבוּ, *You* [plural] *shall not steal*, and that refers to the stealing of money and property.

That our verse indicates kidnapping, rather than theft, is indicated by its context. The Sages teach (*Sanhedrin* 87a) that because the preceding sins are murder and adultery, both of which are capital offenses, we must assume that *You shall not steal* also involves a form of theft that can make its perpetrator liable to the death penalty. The only such theft is kidnapping, as we find in *Exodus* 21:16: *One who steals a man and sells him ... shall surely die.* The death penalty is incurred only if the kidnapper forces his victim to serve him like a slave, and then sells him (*Rambam; Hil. Geneivah* 9:2).

The commentators pose an intriguing question as to the choice of words in this commandment. In common Scriptural usage, the root גנב, *thievery*, is used to indicate burglary or other stealthy theft, while גזל, *robbery*, is used to describe brazen stealing in the victim's presence. Accordingly, the appropriate term here would seem to be לא תגזל, *you shall not rob [by force]*, since the victim is forcibly seized.

R' Bezalel Ashkenazi (Responsa 39) explains that the victim of kidnapping is not only the person being abducted, but the family — father, mother, brothers, sisters, and relatives from whom he is taken. Since *they* are unaware of the crime while it is happening the root גנב is appropriate.

Sforno observes that although the context proves that the prohibition refers mainly to kidnapping (see above), this commandment also includes ordinary thievery and deception.

The *Midrash* [see *Torah Sheleimah*] explains the reason for the singular form לא תגנב in the Ten Commandments and the plural לא תגנבו in *Lev.* 19:11: The Torah warns us not to steal either individually or in concert with others. The two verses allude to both forms of stealing.

[Under the seven Noachide laws, theft refers only to the taking of another person's property or causing direct monetary loss. The scope of the Torah prohibition, however, exceeds these narrow limits and makes straight demands upon the Jew to be painstakingly scrupulous with the possessions of others. In business affairs the Torah demands complete integrity and conduct that is above all suspicion or reproach. Some examples are:

□ Not only is it forbidden to take excessive profit, it is also forbidden to lend money to a fellow Jew for interest, and the lender is called a *robber (Bava Metzia* 62a).

□ The Torah's extreme sensitivity to the value of personal dignity is evidenced by the Talmudic dictum that if someone greets his neighbor, and the greeting is not acknowledged, the inconsiderate neighbor is deemed a robber, for having deprived his friend of the courteous response that was due him!

□ Furthermore, we are enjoined to respect the intellectual possessions of our neighbors. If a person presents someone else's idea in his own name, it is similar to stealing (*Tanchuma Bamidbar; Magen Avraham* to *Orach Chaim* 156; *Yalkut Shimoni*, II:960).

□ Finally, it is even forbidden to 'steal' someone's opinion or feelings [גנבת דעת]. This involves deceiving someone — by word or deed — to have a higher opinion of us, or to make someone feel grateful to us, when we are undeserving. Conse-

לֹא
לֹא-

יד תַעֲנֶה בְרֵעֲךָ עֵד שָׁקֶר:
תַחְמֹד בֵּית רֵעֶךָ

quently, it is forbidden to issue an invitation that we know will be rejected, if the invitation is only to curry favor, but is not sincere (*Chullin* 94a).]

Shulchan Aruch warns us that it is prohibited even to buy stolen goods, for if a thief would know that he is unable to sell stolen property, he might not steal any more. Similarly it is forbidden to help someone steal [for example, to serve as a lookout, or to drive someone to or from the scene of the crime] (*Choshen Mishpat* 356:71).

Yerushalmi (Sanhedrin 1:5) sums up: The accomplice of the thief is like the thief himself!

This Commandment — the third to appear on the second tablet — corresponds to the Third Commandment on the first tablet: *You shall not take the Name of HASHEM your God in a vain oath.* Mechilta explains that whoever steals will eventually come to swear in vain [i.e. falsely]. The prophet (*Hoshea* 4:2) equates a thief with one who swears falsely, saying: *There is swearing, and lying, and killing and stealing, and committing adultery.*

**◄§ Ninth Commandment:
Prohibition against bearing false witness**

לֹא-תַעֲנֶה בְרֵעֲךָ עֵד שָׁקֶר — *You shall not bear false witness against your neighbor.*

God said to Israel, 'My nation, do not bear false witness against your neighbor. Do not consort nor deal with those who give false testimony. Keep your children from their company lest they learn from

their wicked deeds. As a punishment for the crime of false testimony, the sky becomes darkened by clouds, yet there is no rain for the crops. Famine stalks the earth' (*Targum Yonasan*).

It is possible to transgress this commandment even if someone gives testimony which he wholeheartedly believes to be the truth. *Rambam (Eidus* 17:13) rules that even if one hears from many great and pious men that someone committed a crime or borrowed money, he may not testify regarding the event. Hearsay evidence is unacceptable no matter how unimpeachable the source.

The Talmud (*Shavuos* 31a) takes this idea a step further and describes the following scenario: A devoted disciple is approached by his teacher who says, 'You know that I would not lie even if I were paid a hundred zuz. Someone owes me a hundred zuz, but denies his debt and I have only one witness. I ask of you only that you accompany my witness to the court and stand with him. When my debtor sees *two* people come to court, he may be afraid that you both will testify against him, and admit his lie'. The Talmud rules that the disciple who participates in this deception transgresses the commandment: *You shall not bear false witness.*

The above ruling explains why our verse reads לֹא תַעֲנֶה, literally, *you shall not answer* or *repeat*, instead of the more straightforward לֹא תָעִיד, *you shall not testify.* The wording alludes to the prohibition

You shall not bear false witness against your neighbor.

¹⁴ *You shall not covet your neighbor's house.*

against the *repetition* of hearsay — even if true — by someone who did not actually witness the event (*Haamek Davar*).

Meshech Chochmah uses the same principle to resolve a difficulty posed by *Ibn Ezra*. Why does the verse not speak of עֵדוּת שֶׁקֶר, *false testimony*, instead of mentioning only the עֵד, *witness*, who testifies? In view of the above dictum however, the 'testimony' could indeed be true and the 'witness' false, for someone who testifies from hearsay is regarded as עֵד שֶׁקֶר, *a false witness*, even though what he says is true.

In the second version (*Deuteronomy* 5:17) the text reads: לֹא תַעֲנֶה בְרֵעֲךָ עֵד שָׁוְא, *You shall not bear 'vain' witness against your neighbor*. *Ramban* explains that the changed expression adds that a witness may not testify untruthfully even if his testimony will cause no financial loss to anyone. For example, an expression of mere *intent* to give a gift is not binding. Consequently, even if it were proven that such an intention had been expressed, the potential giver would retain the right to change his mind. Nevertheless, although testimony regarding such a statement would not cause anyone a loss, the testimony would be 'vain' and should not be made in court.[1]

This Commandment — the fourth on the second tablet — corresponds to the Fourth Commandment on the first tablet: *Remember the Sabbath day to sanctify it*. Rabbi Yossi taught: The Sabbath is a day when Israel testifies that God created the world by saying: *In six days HASHEM made the heaven and the earth ... and He rested on the seventh day*. Whoever desecrates the Sabbath denies the truth of this testimony and bears false witness against all the teachings of the Torah (*Mechilta*).

⋰§ **Tenth Commandment:**
Prohibition against coveting

14. לֹא תַחְמֹד בֵּית רֵעֶךָ — *You shall not covet your neighbor's house*.

God said to Israel, 'My nation, do not covet what is not yours. Do not consort or mingle with people who covet. Prevent your children from entering their company lest they learn from their evil ways. When this commandment is violated the government treats its subjects harshly both physically and economically. The wealthy lose their possessions and exile comes to the world (*Targum Yonasan*).

In the second version (*Deutero-*

---

1. Since even 'vain' testimony is forbidden, why does the verse in *Exodus* forbid only *false* testimony, implying that vain witness would be permitted? The first time the Ten Commandments were given — before the sin of the Golden Calf — Israel was at such a high level of integrity that even a non-binding expression of intent would be honored as though it were an unalterable obligation. Consequently, proof of such an expression of intent indeed had standing in *beis din*, and was not *vain* in the least. As a result of the sin, however, Israel's level of integrity fell to a lower degree, and people were less scrupulous to honor a non-binding promise (*Kli Chemdah*).

תַחְמֹד אֵשֶׁת רֵעֶךָ וְעַבְדּוֹ וַאֲמָתוֹ וְשׁוֹרוֹ וַחֲמֹרוֹ וְכֹל אֲשֶׁר לְרֵעֶךָ:

nomy 5:18) the wording is: לֹא תִתְאַוֶּה בֵּית רֵעֶךָ, *You shall not desire your neighbor's house.*

Rambam (Gezeilah 1:9,10) explains the difference between תַּאֲוָה and חֶמְדָּה [which we translate, for lack of equivalent English words, as *desire* and *covetousness*]. Whoever desires his friend's house, wife, or possessions transgresses *you shall not desire* from the moment he begins to meditate on how he can achieve his goal. If, however, his desire becomes so intense that he urges and cajoles the owner to sell it to him — and he succeeds in consummating the purchase, he transgresses *you shall not covet*, even though he paid a good price. [Thus, *desire* refers to an unrealized wish, while covetousness refers to a desire that is realized.]

However, *Ravad* holds that the transgression against coveting is not violated if the owner sells willingly.

R' Yonah writes that if you desire to buy an article belonging to someone who does not want to sell it, but he will be ashamed to refuse your request to buy it, you are forbidden to make the request; it would be tantamount to forcing him to sell the article.

Similarly, if a respected person desires something and knows that because people respect him he will not be refused, he may not ask the owner of the article to sell or give it to him unless he knows that the person will do so willingly *(Shaarei Teshuva 3:43)*.

Someone who uses physical force to take away an object from its owner and then reimburses him for

this article, is termed a חַמְסָן, *violent robber,* and is disqualified to testify as is an ordinary thief *(Bava Kamma 62a).*

Rambam (Gezeilah 1:11) warns that desire leads to coveting which in turn can lead to stealing, because if the owner of the desired article remains adamant and refuses to sell it, the one who covets may well steal it outright if he has lost control over himself. This is as the prophet *(Michah 2:2)* warned, *They will covet houses and then steal them.* If the owners stand up to him to protect their property, the covetous person may even go so far as to kill to realize his desire, as Ahab did to Naboth. [Ahab, King of Israel, desired the vineyard of Naboth who refused to sell it and accept another one in exchange. Jezebel, Ahab's wicked wife, hired two people to bear false witness against Naboth, accusing him of blaspheming God. As a result, Naboth was put to death, enabling Ahab to confiscate the field for himself *(I Kings,* chap. 21).]

This Commandment, the fifth on the second tablet, corresponds to the Fifth Commandment on the first tablet: *Honor your father and mother,* because the person who covets what belongs to others will bear a child who will dishonor him *(Mechilta).*

Kli Yakar explains homiletically that someone who covets the property of others will surely be tight-fisted with his own. That sort of person can hardly be expected to support his parents generously. Learning from his example, his

You shall not covet your neighbor's wife, nor his manservant, nor his maidservant, nor his ox, nor his ass, nor anything that is your neighbor's.

children will ignore him as well. If he is in need, he can expect them to say, 'If you need money so badly, go out and beg for it!'

Furthermore, if a person covets another man's wife, it can have spiritual complications for his own marriage causing him to give birth to children who will bring him misery.

Since it is human nature to desire attractive objects, one may reasonably wonder how it is possible to avoid transgressing this sin.

Ibn Ezra explains that the key to self-control lies in attaining a proper perspective on the concept of ownership and acquisition. He illustrates the point with the parable of a poor peasant who sees the lovely princess for the first time. As beautiful as she is, the peasant would never dream of marrying her. Her status is so far above his that such thought never enters his mind; she is utterly unapproachable. The man of faith should train his mind to think of acquisition in the same terms. One must believe that whatever man acquires is a direct gift of God Who determines every person's needs and supplies them. No one can interfere with this Divine decision, nor can he divert by even a hairsbreadth from that which is ordained for another (*Yoma* 38b). When someone realizes that his neighbor's fortunes are completely divorced from those of all other men, it will never enter his mind to desire them.

Similarly no man develops a lust for his own mother no matter how attractive she may be. From the moment he is born, he knows that she is forbidden to him so any desire for her is banished from his mind.

Therefore, says *Meam Loez*, a person should contemplate soberly and reason with himself: God is the Master of my fate, not I. If I deserve to own something, surely He will not withhold it from me. But if something is not destined to be mine then all of my pains and efforts to acquire it will come to naught. So, it is futile to pursue it.

Based on this concept, *Kad HaKemach* observes that the First and the Tenth Commandments are interdependent and interrelated. A person who believes firmly in *I* [alone] *am HASHEM your God* will not question His providence and will experience no desire for that which God bequeathed to another. But someone who covets another man's property will eventually question and even deny God's sovereignty.

Ha'Kesav VeHakabbalah sees another relationship between these commandments: One who contemplates the first commandment and comprehends even a bit of God's greatness and goodness is filled with a love and yearning to come even closer to the Almighty. The man who becomes obsessed with a burning passion for his Maker has no room in his heart to covet another's belongings.

לֹא תַחְמֹד אֵשֶׁת רֵעֶךָ וְעַבְדּוֹ וַאֲמָתוֹ וְשׁוֹרוֹ וַחֲמֹרוֹ — *You shall not covet your neighbor's wife, nor his manservant, nor his maidservant, nor his ox, nor his ass.*

Ibn Ezra comments that the list follows the logical sequence of normal human ambition. An intelligent person will first acquire a house, then marry a wife, and only afterwards acquire servants. But in the second version (*Deuteronomy* 5:18) the wife is mentioned before a house, because young men desire to marry before acquiring a house. *Ramban* comments that *wife* may have been put at the head of the list because to covet someone else's wife is the greatest sin of all things mentioned in this sequence.

R' Bachya explains that the Torah enumerates a list of objects not to be coveted to emphasize that it is reprehensible only to yearn for another man's *material* wealth, but it is quite proper to envy another's *spiritual* attainments, as the Talmud (*Bava Basra* 22a) teaches: קִנְאַת סוֹפְרִים תַּרְבֶּה חָכְמָה, *jealousy among Torah scholars increases wisdom.* When a scholar sees how much knowledge his peer has acquired, the example will prod him to greater efforts to augment his own store of wisdom.

The second version also inserts an item not found here: שָׂדֵהוּ, *his* [your neighbor's] *field. Rokeach* explains that the first version was given in the wilderness where there were no fields to covet. The second version, however, was destined to be recorded in *Deuteronomy,* the book that was given in the fortieth year of Israel's sojourn as they camped just across the Jordan from the Promised Land and productive fields awaited them. Thus, in the second version it became necessary to include this item. [Presumably, *your neighbor's house* in the first version would refer to the tents in the wilderness.]

וְכֹל אֲשֶׁר לְרֵעֶךָ — *Nor anything that is your neighbor's.*

[This word וְכֹל may be rendered *everything,* implying that we are enjoined from coveting the *entire* fortune of a neighbor. This may be interpreted homiletically as an explanation of why it is foolish to covet another man's fortune. Before growing envious of an individual object or talent that someone else enjoys, take inventory of *everything* that he has; his possessions, lifestyle, family, and so on. In all probability, his problems will balance out his good fortune. If he lives in a luxurious home, he may have a shrewish wife. If his wife is a wonderful person, he may have business difficulties. If his business is thriving, you may pity him for his health problems. The possibilities are endless. When you become aware of *everything that is your neighbor's* you will cease to envy him, realizing that God gave him his luxuries to compensate for his woes and to lighten his burden.

A folk parable tells of a group of people gathered in a circle. They throw down their respective packs of woes into a pile in the center, and each one is given the opportunity to exchange his burden for any other one. They all examine the variety of burdens available to them — and each one decides to take back his own bundle.]

Kad HaKemach stresses that not only is it prohibited to covet *anything that is your neighbor's* but it is even forbidden to 'covet' your own possessions, i.e., do not love even your *own* money *too* much, because greed will cripple your judgment and reduce you to a tight-fisted, moral invalid who cannot open his hand to charity. By placing the prohibition against coveting as the tenth of the commandments, the

Torah intended it to be a reminder that a Jew must give a tenth of his earnings to charity. Let the potentially greedy person remember that a part of his resources belongs to the poor — and not covet too much for himself.

The Rabbis provided additional warnings to underline the pitfalls of covetousness, saying: Whenever someone casts his gaze upon that which does not belong to him, the object of his desire will not be granted to him and that which he already possesses will be taken away from him. Coveting is truly the root of all evil, for it caused the very first sin, as it says (Genesis 3:6), And the woman saw that the tree was good for eating and that it was a delight to the eyes and that the tree was desirable [וְנֶחְמָד הָעֵץ] as

a means to wisdom and she took of its fruit and ate.

The serpent coveted Eve, the wife of Adam. The object of the serpent's desire was denied him and he also lost that which he originally possessed. At first the serpent walked upright like man and enjoyed the exalted position of King of the Beasts. But after he sinned, he was stripped of his sovereignty and of his legs, and was cursed to slither ignominiously on his belly for all time.

The same fate awaited all the other villains who cast their envious eyes on the belongings of others: Cain, Korach, Balaam, Doeg, Achitophel, Gechazi, Absalom, Adoniyahu, Uzihayu and Haman (Sotah 9a-b; Bereishis Rabbah 20:10).

R' Saadiah Gaon shows that all 613 mitzvos are alluded to in the Ten Commandments. Others say that every positive mitzvah falls under the category of the First Commandment — to believe in God's existence and power — because every positive mitzvah brings us closer to God. Every negative mitzvah falls under the category of the Second Commandment, because every transgression removes us from a perfect faith in God; in this sense it is akin to idolatry. Consequently, the Ten Commandments may be viewed as containing the fundamentals of Judaism.

The Talmud (Berachos 12a) relates that the Rabbis once considered introducing the recital of the Ten Commandments as part of the Shema liturgy, because, like the Shema, they are a basic declaration of the Jewish faith. However, the practice was discontinued because of the מִינִים, heretics, who maliciously cited the proposed practice as proof that only the Ten Commandments were given by God at Sinai, but not the rest of the Torah. Nevertheless, Yerushalmi (Berachos 1:5) demonstrates how each of the Ten Commandments is alluded to in the words of the Shema itself:

□ I am HASHEM, your God is echoed in שְׁמַע יִשְׂרָאֵל ה' אֱלֹהֵינוּ, Hear Israel, HASHEM is our God;

□ You shall not recognize the gods of others is paralleled by ה' אֶחָד, HASHEM is One, the only One;

□ You shall not take the Name of HASHEM ... in a vain oath coincides with וְאָהַבְתָּ אֵת ה' אֱלֹהֶיךָ, You shall love HASHEM, your God — for one who truly loves his king will not swear falsely in his name;

□ Remember the Sabbath day is alluded to in לְמַעַן תִּזְכְּרוּ, so that you shall remember and do all of my mitzvos — for Scripture equates Sabbath observance with the fulfillment of the totality of all mitzvos, 'Your holy Sabbath did You make known to them, and mitzvos, decrees and Torah did You command them' (Nehemiah 9:14);

□ Honor your father and mother so that you may live a long life is found in לְמַעַן יִרְבּוּ, that your days and the days of your children may be increased;

□ You shall not kill, if transgressed, will be punished by וַאֲבַדְתֶּם מְהֵרָה, you will be swiftly destroyed — for he who kills shall be killed;

□ *You shall not commit adultery* can only be adhered to if you obey לֹא תָתוּרוּ, *you shall not be led astray after your heart and your eyes* — for these organs are the *agents provocateur* of sin [the eyes see and the heart desires];

□ *You shall not steal* from another is reflected in וְאָסַפְתָּ דְגָנֶךָ, *you will gather 'your' wheat,* — your own wheat and not your neighbor's;

□ *You shall not bear false witness,* rather you shall follow in the paths of ה' אֱלֹהֵיכֶם אֱמֶת, *HASHEM, your God, who is Truth;* and

□ *You shall not covet your neighbor's house* is implied in the *mitzvah* of *mezuzah* which is *on the doorpost of 'your' house,* — your own house, not your neighbor's.

Thus, whoever recites the *Shema* daily is, in effect, affirming the Ten Commandments as well.

The fact that God presented His fundamental commands in ten statements also has significance. Because the number ten alludes to the עֲשָׂרָה מַאֲמָרוֹת, *ten utterances* with which God created the world *(Avos 5:1)*, adherence to the Ten Commandments assures the continuity and future existence of the world.

Furthermore, God demonstrated His total mastery over nature and man when He visited ten plagues upon the Egyptians. Since the Almighty alone is Master of the Universe we are obligated to fulfill His commands *(Pesikta Rabbasi 21)*.

תם ונשלם שבח לאל בורא עולם